Wineing Your Way Across INDIANA

Recipes, History, and Scenery

WRITTEN BY BECKY KELLEY

PHOTOGRAPHY BY

MOLLY KELLEY & KATHY WOODHOUSE

Acclaim Press
— Your Next Great Book —

P.O. Box 238
Morley, MO 63767
(573) 472-9800
www.acclaimpress.com

Cover Photography: Molly Kelley
Book Design: Rodney Atchley
Cover Design: M. Frene Melton

ISBN: 978-1-942613-60-2 | 1-942613-60-1
Library of Congress Control Number: 2016917626

First Printing 2017
Printed in the United States of America
10 9 8 7 6 5 4 3 2 1

This publication was produced using available information.
The publisher regrets it cannot assume responsibility for errors or omissions.

Contents

Dedications

First, I would like to thank all of the wineries who generously opened their doors to us so that we may bring to the people their stories of each unique winery in Indiana. I would like to thank the team at Purdue who work so hard to help the wineries and ensure that wineries once again are part of Indiana's valued history. I learned something new from each one of you and for that, you have my unending appreciation. I also thank my partners on this book, Kathy Woodhouse and Molly Kelley. I'm glad you like to turn the radio up and sing off key as much as I do. I need to thank our husbands, Tony Kelley and Mike Woodhouse, and fiancé, Tyler Finley, for their unending support in helping us to complete this project. Your storytelling, driving, and roles as food tasters, helped us immeasurably. Last, I have to thank to writing friends, Jean Kinsey and Diane Theiler, who encouraged me every step of the way. It has been quite a journey and I couldn't imagine sharing it with anyone else.

Salute!
Becky Kelley

Not many people get the chance to work on a labor of love with friends and family. I want to thank my friend, Becky Kelley, for sharing this incredible journey as we Wined Our Way Across Indiana. Thanks also to Becky's daughter, Molly, who stepped in as back-up photographer whenever needed and to Becky's husband, Tony Kelley, for his honest feedback on recipes. His storytelling and quick wit kept us laughing from winery to winery. I learned so much from the hard working, passionate Indiana people; some working two or three jobs, who can live their dreams of being part of this ancient art of winemaking. Each and every winery and vineyard we visited taught us new lessons as we heard the great stories each had to tell. I want to thank all of them for being so open and accepting of us. Finally, I want to thank my husband, Mike, who has stood by me, encouraged me, inspired me, but most of all believed in me. Without his support, this book wouldn't have been possible. I hope you enjoy Wineing Your Way Around Indiana as much as we did.

Cheers!
Kathy Woodhouse

First, I would like to thank my mother, Becky Kelley, for inviting me to work with her on this outstanding, beautiful book. It was a fantastic adventure and I'm so glad that we've connected like never before. I would also like to thank Kathy Woodhouse, an excellent creative photographer, her husband, Mike Woodhouse, and my father, Tony Kelley, for all placing their trust in me to accomplish this difficult task. They never doubted I could do it, so I didn't doubt myself. I want to thank my fiancé for supporting me and giving me his opinions, most of which were honest. I want to thank every winery, every winemaker, and every winery owner, for this delicious learning experience. You have taught me far more than you know. I want to thank all my animal photography subjects; you were all great models and fun to work with. I want to thank my cats for being understanding when their dinner was late, which happened a lot. They, and so many others, supported me in my wineing activities. I could not have imagined the fun, dirty, hot, cold, work that lay ahead when I took on this project, and I can't wait for the next one. I hope all of you like the efforts.

Cheers!
Molly Kelley

Foreword

This book, *Wineing Your Way Across Indiana*, captures a moment in time, of a wonderful and rapidly changing industry. The romance of wineries and vineyards are undeniable. Vineyards present to us a vision of nature tamed, while the wines from the cellars let us experience great flavors and aromas that stimulate our memory and talk to us about the earth and the seasons. In this book the beautiful pictures by Molly Kelley and Kathy Woodhouse go a long way in exploring Indiana wine and bring out the beauty of the experience. The text by Becky Kelley adds depth and vitality to these visual images and conveys to us some of her personal interaction with the people and places she has visited. Hopefully when you read this book you will say to yourself, "I want to be there".

Grape growing and winemaking have deep roots in Indiana. Commercial wine production goes back over 200 years. In fact, it has been argued that the first successful commercial wine production in the United States was in Southeastern Indiana in the small town of Vevay on the Ohio River. Vevay was founded in 1802 by the Dufours, a Swiss winemaking family escaping the havoc of Napoleon's armies. Wine production in Vevay reached its apex in the 1820s. New Harmony, settled by the followers of "Father Rapp", was a German wine producing community in Southwest Indiana from 1814 to about 1825. Italian families established wine making in various areas of the state in the mid and later 1800s. Wineries could be found across Indiana until prohibition all but obliterated them in 1919.

When prohibition ended, Indiana state laws did not favor the reestablishment of wineries. That did not happen until the passage of the Indiana Small Winery Act in 1971. At that time a change was taking place across the country, and state laws governing wineries were becoming more liberal. Since then the number of wineries has grown steadily. The authors visited almost every winery open at the time of writing. There are even more wineries, not mentioned here, that are "waiting in the wings", yet to open their doors.

It will become obvious to the attentive reader that each winery has its own style and philosophy of wine production. While most years are very favorable for grape growing in Indiana, extreme weather does occur. Dealing with variable temperatures and precipitation keeps the growers and winemakers on their toes, each vintage offering its own challenges and opportunities. A number of different grape varieties are being grown, some commonly known to the consumer and some that are much more mysterious. These wines offer unique character and style that reflect the climate, the land and the people who make the wine. The public is discovering Indiana wines that are fresh, fruit forward and well balanced. The local food movement should be demanding these local wines.

As you read this book, please be aware of all the work that has gone into collecting the wonderful photographs and developing the text that expresses the heart and soul of each winery. And please also remember the years of hard work that grape growing and wine producing families have put into bringing little works of art to your table. I leave it to you to discover the wines of Indiana in your own way and time. I think that *Wineing Your Way Across Indiana* will be a valuable tool in that discovery. Happy travels.

Jim Butler
Butler Winery

Introduction

*H*ello fellow wine lover(s). This guide was created to introduce people to all the wonderful wineries of Indiana and to take the mystery out of wine for those who may not know the supposed "correct" way to enjoy it. The people who created this book wanted everyone to see what a great representation of Indiana's hardworking people, and award winning vintages, these wineries contain. Some of them also have distilleries and/or breweries, so there's something for all taste preferences. Some of them have restaurants with full menus of delicacies and many offer overnight accommodations. Many of the wineries, settled in peaceful surroundings, want to nourish a sense of serenity and balance. Most importantly, all of them want to facilitate good times with wonderful people and an appreciation of Indiana crafted wines.

Wine is one of those things some people tend to avoid. There seem to be a lot of Wine rules which change from red to white and everything in between. However, just as with food, wine should be chosen by preference; there is no such thing as a "wrong" wine. The soil grapes are grown in, nutrients used, and amount of rain and sun, along with a myriad of other factors, will affect the taste of the grape and thus the wine from year to year. According to many of the winery owners, "A good wine is one people like to drink."

Many people like the oaky taste which accompanies some of the dry wines aged in oak barrels, some do not. Some people drink sweet wines alone or with a dessert while others prefer cheeses or other foods that enhance the flavor of both the food and drink. Peoples' taste buds are developed differently based on what a person inherits and what food experiences train his or her likes and dislikes. Previous experiences with wine will also guide a person's preference. A person does not have to know all the supposed rules to enjoy wine, just follow your own tastes and raise a glass or two in friendship and good health. The writer and photographers sincerely hope the people exploring with the help of this guide, have a renewed appreciation for the state as they wine their way around Indiana.

Cheers!

List of Wineries by County

Adams County

Allen County

Bartholomew County
- Best Vineyards Winery (Elizabeth)
- Simmons Winery & 450 North Brewing Co. (Columbus)
- Smith's Winery (Columbus)

Benton County

Blackford County

Boone County
- Hopwood Cellars Winery (Zionsville)

Brown County
- Brown County Winery (Nashville)
- Cedar Creek Winery Tasting Room (Nashville)
- Salt Creek Nashville Tasting Room (Nashville)

Carroll County

Cass County
- Indian Trail Wines (Royal Center)
- The People's Winery (Logansport)

Clark County
- Huber Orchard, Winery & Vineyard (Borden)

Clay County

Clinton County

Crawford County

Daviess County

Dearborn County
- At the Barn Winery (Lawrenceburg)
- Chateau Pomije (Guilford)
- Powers Winery (Dillsboro)

Decatur County

DeKalb County
- Byler Lane Winery (Auburn)
- Hartland (Ashley)

Delaware County
- Tonne Winery (Muncie)

Dubois County
- Monkey Hollow Winery & Bistro at the Wollenmann Home (Ferdinand)
- Patoka Lake (Birdseye)

Elkhart County
- Fruit Hills Winery & Orchard (Bristol)
- Gateway Cellar Winery & Wine Bar (Goshen)

Fayette County

Floyd County
- Indian Creek Winery (Georgetown)
- River City Winery (New Albany)

Fountain County

Franklin County

Fulton County
- Schnabeltier Artisan Cheese & Wine (Rochester)

Gibson County

Grant County
- Oak Hill Winery (Converse)

Greene County

Hamilton County
- Blackhawk Winery (Sheridan)
- Country Moon Winery (Noblesville)
- Harmony Winery (Fishers)
- Peace Water Winery (Carmel)

Hancock County
- Daniel's Vineyard (McCordsville)

Harrison County
- Scout Mountain Winery and Bed & Breakfast (Corydon)
- Turtle Rum Winery (Corydon)

Hendricks County
- Chateau Thomas Winery (Plainfield)
- Quibble Hill Winery (Depauw)

Henry County
- Belgian Horse Winery (Middletown)

Howard County

Huntington County
- Two EE's Winery (Huntington)

Jackson County
- Chateau de Pique (Seymour)
- Salt Creek Winery (Freetown)

Jasper County
- Carpenter Creek Cellars (Remington)

Jay County
- The Tipsy Glass Winery (Bryant)

Jefferson County
- Lanthier Winery (Madison)
- Madison Vineyards Estate Winery and Bed & Breakfast (Madison)
- Thomas Family Winery (Madison)

Jennings County
- Stream Cliff Farm (Commiskey)

Johnson County
- Mallow Run Winery (Bargersville)
- River City Winery Franklin Tasting Room (Franklin)

Knox County
- Windy Knoll Winery (Vincennes)

Kosciusko County
- Tippy Creek Winery (Leesburg)

LaGrange County

Lake County

LaPorte County
- Shady Creek Winery (Michigan City)

Lawrence County
- Carousel Winery (Mitchell)

Madison County
- Madison County Winery & Vineyard (Markleville)

Marion County
- Ash & Elm Cider Co. (Indianapolis)
- Buck Creek (Indianapolis)
- Chateau de Pique Tasting Room (Indianapolis)
- Easley Winery (Indianapolis)
- New Day Craft (Indianapolis)
- Traders Point Winery (Indianapolis)

Marshall County

Martin County

Miami County
- McClure's Orchard & Winery (Peru)

Monroe County
- Butler Winery & Vineyard (Bloomington)
- Butler Winery In-Town Tasting Room (Bloomington)
- Oliver Winery (Bloomington)

Montgomery County
- Coal Creek Cellars (Crawfordville)

Morgan County
- Cedar Creek Winery (Martinsville)

Newton County

Noble County
- Country Heritage Winery & Vineyards (Laotto)

Ohio County
- Fiekert's Homestead Wines (Rising Sun)

Orange County
- French Lick Winery & The Vintage Café (West Baden Springs)

Owen County
- Owen Valley Winery (Spencer)
- Owen Valley Tivoli Theater Tasting Room (Spencer)

Parke County

Perry County
- Blue Heron Vineyards and Bed & Breakfast (Cannelton)
- Winzerwald Winery (Bristow)

Pike County

Porter County
- Aftermath Cidery & Winery (Valparaiso)
- Anderson's Vineyard & Winery (Valparaiso)
- Butler Winery Tasting Room (Chesterton)
- Lambstone Cellars (Valparaiso)
- Missbeehavin Meads (Valparaiso)
- Running Vines Winery (Chesterton)

Posey County
- Hedgegrove Meadery & Winery (Cynthiana)

Pulaski County

Putnam County

Randolph County
- Wilson Wines (Modoc)

Ripley County
- Ertel Cellars (Batesville)
- Holtkamp Winery (Sunman)
- Rettig Hill Winery (Milan)

Rush County

St. Joseph County
- Ironhand Vineyard (South Bend)

Scott County

Shelby County

Spencer County
- Monkey Hollow Winery (St. Meinrad)
- Pepper's Ridge Winery (Rockport)

Starke County

Steuben County
- Briali Vineyards & Winery (Fremont)
- Satek Winery (Fremont)

Sullivan County

Switzerland County
- The Ridge Winery Tasting Room (Vevay)

Tippecanoe County
- Wildcat Creek Winery (Lafayette)

Tipton County

Union County

Vanderburgh County
- Little Creek Winery (Evansville)

Vermillion County
- TJ Haase Winery (Clinton)
- Windy Ridge Vineyard & Winery (Cayuga)

Vigo County

Wabash County
- Heagy Vineyards (Roann)

Warren County

Warrick County
- Mystique Winery (Lynnville)
- Stoney Creek Winery (Millersburg)

Washington County

Wayne County
- J&J Winery (Richmond)

Wells County

White County
- Fruitshine Winery (Monticello)
- Whyte Horse Winery (Monticello)

Whitley County

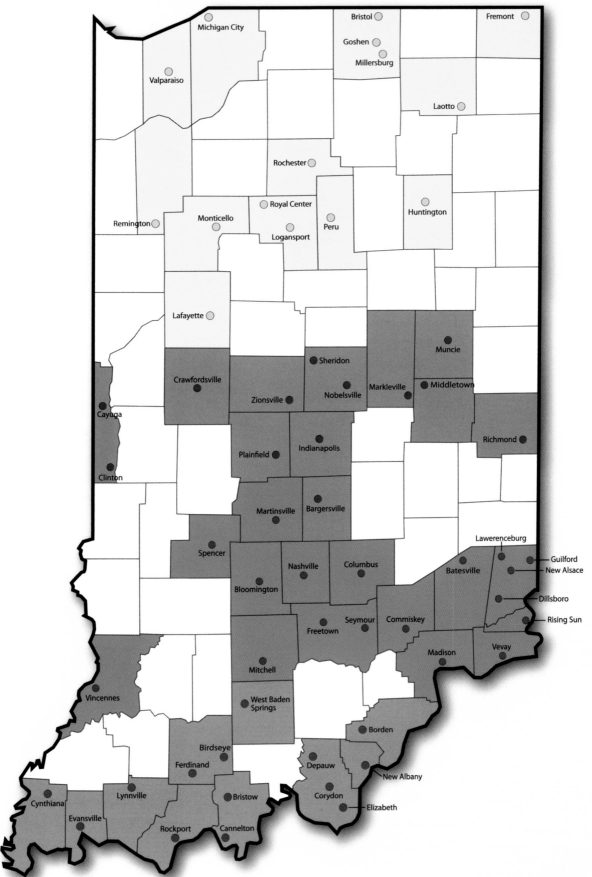

Michigan City

Bristol

Fremont

Valparaiso

Goshen
Millersburg

Laotto

Rochester

Remington
Monticello

Royal Center
Logansport

Peru

Huntington

Lafayette

Muncie

Sheridan

Crawfordsville

Zionsville

Nobelsville

Markleville

Middletown

Cayuga

Plainfield

Indianapolis

Richmond

Clinton

Martinsville

Bargersville

Spencer

Lawerenceburg

Guilford

New Alsace

Nashville

Columbus

Batesville

Bloomington

Dillsboro

Rising Sun

Seymour

Commiskey

Mitchell

Freetown

Madison

Vevay

West Baden
Springs

Borden

Vincennes

Birdseye

Ferdinand

Depauw

New Albany

Cynthiana

Lynnville

Bristow

Corydon

Elizabeth

Evansville

Rockport

Cannelton

9

The Northern Region

WILDCAT CREEK WINERY • *Lafayette, Tippecanoe County*
WHYTE HORSE WINERY • *Monticello, White County*
CARPENTER CREEK CELLARS • *Remington, Jasper County*
ANDERSON'S ORCHARD & WINERY INC. • *Valparaiso, Porter County*
SHADY CREEK WINERY • *Michigan City, Laporte County*
FRUIT HILLS WINERY & ORCHARD • *Bristol, Elkhart County*
GATEWAY CELLAR WINERY • *Goshen, Elkhart County*
STONEY CREEK WINERY • *Millersburg, Elkhart County*
BRIALI WINERY • *Freemont, Steuben County*
SATEK WINERY • *Freemont, Steuben County*
COUNTRY HERITAGE WINERY & VINEYARD • *Laotto, Noble County*
TWO EE'S WINERY • *Huntington, Huntington County*
MCCLURE'S ORCHARD & WINERY • *Peru, Miami County*
SCHNABELTIER ARTISAN CHEESE & WINE • *Rochester, Fulton County*
INDIAN TRAIL WINES • *Royal Center, Cass County*
THE PEOPLE'S WINERY • *Logansport, Cass County*

Additional Wineries
(see page 294 for information)

AFTERMATH CIDERY & WINERY • *219-390-9463*
BYLER LANE WINERY • *260-920-4377*
FRUITSHINE WINERY • *574-808-9229*
HARTLAND WINERY • *260-668-5324*
HEAGY VINEYARDS • *317-752-4779*
IRONHAND VINEYARD • *574-360-5388*
LAMBSTONE CELLARS
OAK HILL WINERY • *765-395-3632*
OAK HILL WINERY "31" TASTING ROOM • *765-395-3632*
RUNNING VINES WINERY • *219-390-9463*
TIPPY CREEK WINERY • *574-529-0469*

WILDCAT CREEK WINERY
NORTH LAFAYETTE

"Hoosier hospitality is first and foremost"
–Kathy and Rick Black

"I was a little scared," admitted Kathy Black when discussing their first adventures when opening Wildcat Creek Winery in 2008. "I was hoping we'd sell a bottle or two a week. After six months, I took home the guest book. We had people from 44 states and 12 countries." Although Wildcat Creek Winery is wildly popular now, it almost didn't happen.

Both of the Blacks had full careers. With Rick's MBA in finance from Indiana University, he'd been a successful financial controller for many different companies. Kathy had a rewarding career as a school teacher. As they were nearing retirement age, they felt a shift in the drive of their day to day lives, and wanted to move toward something new and different. It was while visiting wineries that the idea struck that this is what they wanted; but they had no idea how to go about it.

In 2000, Kathy and Rick started a search for some ground to start a winery. "I was an amateur," explained Rick. "I didn't have the product, the process, or know the industry before I started the business." After seven years of trying to find the perfect place for their dream, the Blacks had stopped looking. Then, they happened to drive by a small farm that was for sale by the owner. After looking at the 1900s' farmhouse with a large front porch and expansive views, they knew they'd found their winery.

Although the Blacks didn't know much about the wine industry, during the years they were looking for the ground, they willingly learned the business and were lucky enough to live near Purdue University. With an enologist, viticulturist, and marketing specialist, it's the hub for all wineries in the state of Indiana. They volunteered to be in the pit crew at the Indy International Wine Competition, and closely observed how the wine was evaluated. With some help from other winery owners and the people at Purdue, they learned about making wine and the winery business.

In 2002 Rick entered his first wine in the amateur division of the Indy International Wine Competition and won "Indiana Amateur Wine Champion." After that, the Blacks were fully committed to becoming winery owners. They felt like they were experiencing little nudges that let them know they were moving in the right direction.

"I would come home from school," Kathy laughed, "and there would be three wine glasses set up for a bench trial. 'Taste this,' Rick would say. 'You know what you like.'" These trials have led to twelve core wines they carry all of the time, plus special editions added in from time to time, including a special edition blueberry created especially for Indiana's 200 year anniversary as a state. "We bottled almost 60 cases and sold out in one day." This was the day of their celebration when almost 1,000 people came to the party. Husband and wife are quick to point to the other as the reason for their success

"Kathy makes decisions about landscaping, products in the tasting room, hiring employees, and selecting paint colors," said Rick. "I make decisions about winemaking and take care of the financial responsibilities; it's been a great partnership."

Kathy added: "Our son David said, 'You have a rustic and elegant tasting room. Dad's the rustic and you're the elegant.' We complement each other," Kathy added. "Life is too short to do something you don't enjoy." Obviously, they both enjoy each other's company and experiencing all owning a winery has to offer. "The business is living, breathing and pulls you in more and more. We love it," exclaimed Kathy. Although they go to extra measures to create incredible wine and a beautiful space, enjoyment of the customer is their first priority.

"Aunt Minnie's Cherry Tree wine is named after my aunt," Kathy continued. "She always made visitors feel so special. It's really important that people experience the Hoosier hospitality and that they feel like a million bucks." That we did as we left the winery with a huge smile. We invite you to visit Wildcat Creek Winery so you can experience it too.

Note: Photographs for Wildcat Creek Winery were provided by Brent Russell.

Wildcat Creek Winery
3233 East 200
North Lafayette, IN 47905
765-838-3498

Events: Yes, after hours, up to 25 indoor or out.

Wines

Prophet's Rock Red
Full-tasting red with flavors of berry and hints of vanilla and oak. Pairs well with traditional Spanish dishes like Paella and red meats, as well as red pasta sauces.

Cayuga White
Subtle flavors of pear, apricot, melon, peach, and apple. Pair with wood-fired cheese pizza, a fruit salad, or ham salad.

Steuben
A delicate, crisp blush wine with cranberry and strawberry flavors and aromas. This easy sipping wine was voted 2012's Indiana Grown American Wine of the Year.

Bicentennial Blueberry
Named in honor of Indiana's 200th anniversary of statehood. This mid-harvest wine has a deep blueberry color and a natural sweetness.

From the Winery

Blueberry Bar-B-Q Sauce

1 cup of Wildcat Creek Bicentennial Blueberry wine
2 cups catsup
1 small onion diced
1 clove of garlic chopped
2 teaspoons chili powder
1 teaspoon cumin
1 teaspoon paprika
¼ cup brown sugar
2 tablespoons balsamic vinegar
½ teaspoon ground coffee
1 small jalapeño pepper diced
1 pint of fresh blueberries

Add all of the ingredients into a pot and simmer for two hours. Use as is or blend and strain. Perfect on chicken or ribs.

Wildcat Creek Blueberry Lemonade

1 part Wildcat Creek Bicentennial Blueberry wine
2 parts lemonade
Garnish with fresh lemon slices and blueberries
Wildcat Creek Blueberry Wine Spritzer
3 parts Wildcat Creek Bicentennial Blueberry wine
1 part mango juice
Top with sparkling water
Garnish with fresh fruit such as berries, mangos, or peaches

WHYTE HORSE WINERY
MONTICELLO

"From wooden stem to crystal stem"
–The Pampels

Whyte Horse Winery is truly a family business with four generations helping with different aspects of all that goes into running a winery. "We are blessed to have part-time employees, and family and friends who love working with us in the tasting room, at festivals, and in the vineyard whenever we have the need."

Whyte Horse Winery got its name after part owners Larry and Connie Pampel bought a farm. They were looking for a new home with woods and a lake or stream for their family to enjoy. They first saw the property along Big Creek in White County, while driving to dinner one evening. They made an appointment to see it, but were told the owners already had a full-price offer. They visited the property, then made a back-up offer, certain they were going to lose this ideal spot. The next day, the owner called. "Will you take the horse?" The 25-year-old white mare was a fixture at the farm and the owner could not take her. The other couple did not want to take the horse. The Pampels agreed to take her and their offer was accepted. "Molly became an important

16

part of our grandchildren's lives," said Larry. "And we all loved being at the farm.

Three years later, while teaching Sunday school classes with Bruce Wilkinson's book, The Secret of the Vine, Connie and Larry sat on the deck looking out at their rolling pasture land. "I want to plant a vineyard," declared Larry. "I want to care for the vines and the fruit." Larry had always had a passion for wine, traveling the world and sampling vintages, so planting a vineyard felt like a natural extension of his travels and agricultural background. Since Larry came from a farm family, they approached his brother Don and his wife Denise, inviting them to be a part of the project. With all in agreement, the search for a property began.

The Pampels found a large parcel of land on the south side of Monticello, but the 1880s' farmhouse that sat on the property posed a bit of a problem. Larry wanted to tear it down, but Connie saw the beauty in the structure and used her gift of decorating to turn the house into a showplace. They chose the name of the winery to honor

Whyte Horse Winery
1510 South Airport Road
Monticello, IN 47960
574-583-3245

Events: Yes, indoors up to 70;
outdoors up to 200

the horse that came with the other farm, and changed the spelling to the give it an old world feel, which is the style of wines Whyte Horse produces.

"They're old world and dry aged in oak barrels," said employee Jackie Kibler. There are also semi-dry and sweet styles aged in stainless steel, so there is something for everyone.

Employee Connie Nolan furthered the idea. "We have a kind of boutique winery where the wines will taste slightly different from year to year, based on climate and weather."

The beautiful property includes the farm house, with porches that wrap nearly all the way around set up with ample seating spaces of bistro style tables and chairs and comfy rockers posed in many places. A majestic gazebo has been the sight of many wedding vows, but also engagements, with special touches added by Connie Nolan. Many activities attract a lot of visitors throughout the year.

There are car shows, sip and paint, fashion shows, facials, vendors, and a very popular event known as the winemakers table. A chef and the winemaker come together to create a special evening of creative foods with wine pairings. Each explains about their choices and how they enhance each other to create a full meal experience.

Another very popular the grape stomp, started in celebration of the har- to thank God, the sea- the weather for their con- to the abundance of the The Pampels invite you to and taste the abundance.

Wines

Chardonnay

Pineapple, banana, lemon, and vanilla with a hint of French oak. This wine pairs well with herb crusted halibut, pork loin, and fresh garden squash casserole.

Malbec

A deep red grape with blackberry and spice aromas, aged in oak, smooth. It pairs well with dark meat poultry or a beef brisket, and garlic mashed potatoes.

Dolce Red

Smooth red blend with rich flavors of plum and chocolate. Pair with pizza, burgers, or hot dogs. This wine isn't pretentious.

Serendipity

This port-style wine is a dessert all by itself, with rich honey and toasted caramel flavors.

Recipe

Pain de Viande avec du Bacon

We thought this was too delicious to call it bacon wrapped meatloaf, so we turned to our English-French dictionary for a little inspiration.

¼ cup of Whyte Horse Chambourcin
1 pound lean ground beef
¼ tsp each of salt, pepper, paprika, onion
    powder, garlic powder, and thyme
½ cup panko crumbs
8 bacon strips

Mix all of the ingredients except the bacon, just until blended. Form into eight equal sized meatloaves. Wrap one piece of bacon around each loaf and set in metal cake pan. Turn oven to 375°.

Sauce

    ¼ cup Whyte Horse Chambourcin
    ½ cup ketchup
    3 Tbl. Brown sugar
    2 Tbl. Worchester sauce

Mix all ingredients and divide in half. Pour half over the meatloaves and the other half into a small saucepan.

Bake meatloaves for 30 minutes. Turn broiler on and cook 1-2 minutes to crisp up the bacon. Heat reserved sauce in pan to boiling. Pour over meatloaves and serve. A family favorite.

CARPENTER CREEK CELLARS
REMINGTON

"Rich with Heritage"
–The Courtrights and Rottlers

The Carpenter Creek Cellar's motto, "Rich with Heritage", comes from the fact that the land it sits on is farmed by the third generation of family to produce an agricultural product. The spacious barn tasting room was originally built in 1919 by the owner, Ed Courtright's, grandfather. Courtright described the process of taking the barn from a place that used to hold draft horses to the pristine vintage look it has today as the barn's "midlife crisis." When entering, be sure to look down at the compass on the concrete stamped and painted floor; it's beautiful. Carpenter Creek Cellars became the first winery in Jasper County, Indiana once the resurgence of the wine industry started in the state. It was a long journey for co-owners Randy and Marilyn Rottler and Ed and Beckie Courtright, from the beginning of an inkling of an idea to opening a winery.

Randy Rottler first became interested in wine while in the Air Force. He traveled throughout Ger-

many and the beauty of the vineyards drew him in. He especially liked the wine region around the Mosel River. The area is known for the steep slopes of the Rhineland vineyards, which overlook the river. He decided then he wanted to own a winery – it just took 40 years to see the dream through.

After his experiences in Germany, Rottler returned home and started to visit wineries around the United States with his wife, Marilyn, making many friends in the wine industry. Randy began making his own wine and playing with different fruits and combinations to see what would develop in the process. While cultivating his interest in wine making, his hobby became a passion and he decided to make it his work, too. Randy noticed grapes growing on nearby land and did some research.

Ed and Beckie Courtright bought the farm started by his grandfather and worked it in traditional farming until retiring. When they decided to downsize, they sold all but ten acres, keeping the house and barn, and planted grapes. Not long after, they received a call.

Randy Rottler was assistant wine maker at another winery, when he googled the acreage where the Courtrights were growing grapes. He called and introduced himself and they began working together to develop wines for the new winery. Rottler and Courtright formed a partnership with Rottler as the winemaker and Courtright as the viticulturist. A viticulturist cultivates the art of growing grapes,

Carpenter Creek Cellars
11144 Jordan Road
Remington, IN 47977
219-866-4334

Events: Yes, up to 60, plus a deck
that holds 20. No weddings.

which is part science and part intuition. After years of paperwork, planning, construction, more planning, and more paperwork, Carpenter Creek Cellars opened to the public on March 23, 2013.

There's a tradition with naming wineries and wines after something pertaining to the area or someone special who has passed. Visitors to the winery may notice two wines called Gunny Red and Gunny White. Gunny was the winery dog before the winery ever existed. This 110 pound Doberman was right there during all the building and planning, but unfortunately passed away shortly before the winery opened. He was so much a part of the process of getting the winery ready, the owners decided to honor him with two separate wines.

In addition to the wonderful wines, Carpenter Creek Winery folks like to throw parties. Once a month, there's a free concert where they invite everyone who wants to come, to bring food and relax in a country atmosphere with a lot of like-minded people. They'll help you pair a wine with whatever foods you select. Bring a picnic, some friends, some chairs and a sense of fun and prepare to make some memories at Carpenter Creek Cellars.

Wines

❧ Gunny Red

A bold, dry, red wine has a great berry aroma with flavors of raspberry, cherry, and spice with a touch of oak. It pairs best with roast beef, spiced pork, red pasta sauces, and dark chocolate desserts.

❧ Gunny White

A semi-dry blended white with a fruity nose and hints of peaches, grapefruit, pear, and apple on the tongue. It works well with spicy foods, Asian cuisine, and white meats.

❧ Sunset Rosé

This soft, juicy blush has a heavy strawberry note that gives way to hints of citrus and spice. Enjoy with light cheeses and fruits or fruity desserts with a hint of tart.

❧ Sunset Red

Sunset Red is a rich, fruity, semi-sweet red with a deep ruby color and aromas of grapes and berries. Add this wine to red sauces for delightfully complex flavors, or enjoy with rich chocolate desserts.

Recipe

Princess Pink

½ cup Carpenter Creek Cellars Sunset Rosé, chilled
¼ cup Peach Schnapps, room temperature
1 tsp. orange marmalade

    In wine glass, microwave orange marmalade for 20 seconds. Immediately add Schnapps and stir to dissolve marmalade. Add chilled wine. Enjoy.

ANDERSON'S ORCHARD & WINERY, INC.
VALPARAISO

"Giving the customer a truly unique country wine experience"
–The Lundstrom Family

In 1927, the Anderson family saw the promise a spot of land could produce. Just south of the largest sand dunes in the Midwest, on the southernmost tip of Lake Michigan, a ridge formed thousands of years ago during the three great Ice Ages. The ridge is called the Valparaiso Moraine and is the highest point in Northwest Indiana. In this spot, the Anderson family started a roadside fruit stand that grew into a forty acre family attraction spot. In 1993, David Lundstrom and family took over the operation, with an eye toward expanding and coupling the orchard with another product—wine. In 1994, the first estate winery north of Indianapolis was established.

Of the forty acres, fifteen of them are now planted in grapes and 2003 saw Anderson's first Estate Bottled wines. The Lundstrom Family strives to keep the traditions established by the Anderson's and the agricultural past of the land, while looking toward expansion.

"We have a fudge factory and bakery," explained Kathy Lundstrom. The bakery is famous for their collection of strudels, pies, cookies, and especially apple cider donuts during the fall. They bake every day, but when they're gone, they're gone so if baked goods are on your itinerary, be sure to get there early. Fudge is available and visitors can sample flavors to pick a favorite. Visitors can also enjoy wagon rides through the beautiful vineyards and cellar tours. The winery likes to promote a community atmosphere by carrying local handmade crafts, as well as steins, glassware, and homemade

jams and jellies. In addition, they're home to the largest selection of beer and wine making supplies in the Chicagoland area. The winery now boasts nineteen wine varieties, ciders, and sparkling wine.

Sparkling wine could be referred to as American Champagne, as there are a lot of similarities to the popular bubbly wine. Because of the Champagne appellation law, it is illegal in most countries to officially label a product Champagne unless it holds to certain strict standards. For a wine to earn the title, it has to come from a region just outside of Paris, France called Champagne, and can only be made using Chardonnay, Pinot Noir, and Pinot Meunier. Thus, sparkling wines are very similar, but cannot be labeled or called champagne.

Anderson's wine makers have had a lot of experience making a variety of wines. Despite this, they keep coming up with new wines and formulas so there's always something new for customers to try. Whether your goal is to bring the family for some fun experiences, bringing friends for a picnic and wine experience, arranged by the winery, or relaxing and breathing in the country air, Anderson's Orchard & Winery, Inc. can meet every need.

"Nothing more excellent or valuable than wine
was ever granted by the gods to man."
–Plato

Anderson's Orchard & Winery, Inc.
430 E US 6
Valparaiso, IN 46383
219-464-4936

Events: Yes, outdoor only; up to 100.

Wines

❧ No Name Red
Estate bottled Merlot-style wine made from Frontenac grapes, this wine pair with Gorgonzola cheese, ribeye, or beef stew.

❧ Seyval Blanc
A light-bodied semi-dry white, is a very versatile wine that pairs with garlicky Italian fare, pesto dishes, and creamy soups.

❧ Traminette
Titled the Indiana grape, this light and refreshing white is a good all-around wine. It pairs best with shrimp in a spicy sauce, sweet and sour chicken, or heavier fishes.

❧ Red Diamond
Flavors of ripe currants, cranberry, honey, strawberry, tart rhubarb and hints of spice highlight this ice wine. An after dinner dessert wine.

Recipe

Anderson's Orchard & Winery, Inc. Cider Pork Chop Glaze

¼ cup Anderson Dry Hard Apple
  Cider
1 cup brown sugar
⅛ tsp orange peel
⅛ tsp all spice
⅛ tsp ground cinnamon

Warm all the ingredients in a sauce-pan until the sugar is dissolved. Glaze either chicken or pork chops just prior to removing them from the grill. Or, coat them with sauce before and during baking.

SHADY CREEK WINERY
MICHIGAN CITY

"Taste, Relax, and Enjoy!"
–The Andersons

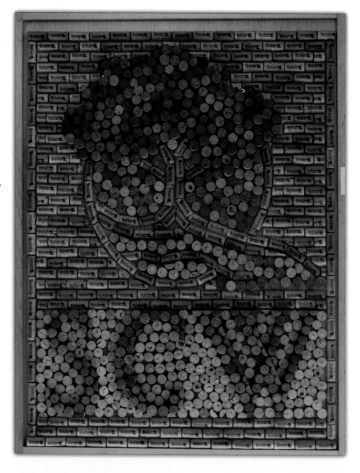

In the beautiful Northwest corner of Indiana, Michigan City sits along a lovely area on the shores of Lake Michigan. Shady Creek Winery chose this spot intentionally for all it had to offer. "The lake, the parks, and other entertainment bring a tremendous amount of visitors to this area," said Tim Anderson, one of the many family members involved with the winery.

The Anderson brothers had a lot of wine experience before they migrated to this area, drawn by the lake lifestyle and the promise of opening a winery. "My interest in wine started when I spent a lot of time on the West Coast for my job," explained Tim. "Making wine became a hobby." He then started counting off siblings. "Mike worked at a winery in Texas, and Jim traveled throughout France. Jerry had a bar and restaurant." The brothers are close and decided they would like to do something together. "I developed the business plan and showed it to everyone," Tim explained. "'Let's go for it' they all said."

Slowly but surely, the whole family is migrating to this enchanting area. Mike is the winemaker, and all the brothers and their spouses are active at the winery. When asked about a typical day, Tim laughed about the lifestyle he so enjoys. "I get up and make the mile commute to work, arriving about nine. I bring the dogs to run around and have fun while I do paperwork. Around eleven, the staff comes in and I hide out until about four when the regular visitors come in. It's taken about seven years to get to the point where I could spend some leisure time with customers."

That's one of Tim Anderson's favorite parts about being part owner in a family winery. "The people who come to the winery are so interesting. They're genuinely interested in all the aspects of what it took to make that particular bottle of wine. They're really interested in the process."

One of the most important decisions when owning a winery is whether to grow grapes and other fruit used in winemaking, buy from local vineyards, or source it from somewhere else. The Anderson's philosophy about this is logical and helped to create their reputation for superb wines. "Because we're a winery and not a vineyard," Tim stressed, "we get to source fruit from the best place for the right wine.

California for the big, dry reds, for example; we're not limited to what we can grow, because we don't grow anything."

This affords the Andersons the opportunity to focus on developing fine wines and excellent customer service. It also allows them to be fully involved in their community, as many of the events held at the winery are local fundraisers.

Whether your goal is excellent service, outstanding wines, great camaraderie, sinking your toes in the sand, or all of them, Shady Creek Winery can provide these to every visitor.

Shady Creek Winery
2030 Tryon Road
Michigan City, IN 46360
219-874-9463

Events: Yes, indoors up to 85; outdoors up to 200

Wines

Beach Glass

A dry white blend of Chardonnel, Pinot Grigio, and Seyval Blanc grapes, hints of citrus and fruit tingle on the tongue. Pair with garlic and orange chicken, smoked salmon with dill, and smoked trout.

Rip Tide

A light red wine blend that has fruit aromas and a complexity of red berry flavors. Pair with cured meats, cheesy potato dishes, and roasted vegetables.

Sandy Feet

A semi-dry white wine blend with floral and grapefruit aromas and flavors of fresh green apples that will delight the senses. Serve chilled.

Red Horizon

A delightfully smooth semi-sweet red wine blend. It has a deep ruby red color and aromas that come from fruits of cherry and blackberry. Serve over your favorite pie.

Recipe

Red, White, and Yum!

¼ cup Shady Creek Winery Red Horizon Wine

¼ cup Shady Creek Winery Beach Glass Wine

1 pound lean ground beef

1 large sweet onion, cut into thick rings

2 cups Italian bread crumbs, divided

2 eggs

½ cup sharp cheddar

1 cup olive oil, heated to 350° in sauce pan deep enough for deep frying

Directions:

Mix red wine, lean ground beef and ½ cup bread crumbs together. Mix eggs and white wine together in a small bowl. In a shallow plate, mix remaining bread crumbs and cheddar cheese.

Fill the onion rings with burger mixture, pressing to fit snuggly into each onion ring. Dip into the egg mixture, then the bread crumb mixture. Fry in the oil until golden brown on each side and until the center is no longer pink, about 2-3 minutes on each side. Serve with favorite burger sauces for dipping, mustard, ketchup, mayonnaise, even barbecue, hot sauce, or horseradish.

FRUIT HILLS WINERY & ORCHARD
BRISTOL

"We want to leave a legacy for our son and grandchildren."
– David and Michele Muir

David and Michele Muir started a winery because they want to continue the legacy that was left to them. The farm was first established in David's family in 1852 and began growing and producing fruit around 1898, and the tradition continues today.

"We've always had a fruit farm here," said David Muir, "and decided to try making wine." He laughingly recalled the early experimentation. "Some were good and some not so good, but since it was on a small scale it didn't hurt us to pour five gallons down the drain."

What pushed the Muirs into opening a winery happened unexpectedly. "In 2009, I lost my town job

and decided to expand the orchard." During a trip to Florida soon after that, they serendipitously decided to stop at a small boutique winery. The Muirs saw that the owners produced their wines from a small room in the back of the winery. At this point, David had been making grape and fruit wines for family for many years, and it was then the idea of the winery first occurred. Things moved along pretty quickly with planning starting that year and the winery opening in 2010.

They've planted three acres of interesting grape varieties such as Petite Pearl, Marquette, and Frontenac Gris. Three acres may not sound like a lot of grapes,

however, one acre of grapes can produce up to around seven thousand bottles of wine, so a little goes a long way with some varieties. The Muirs also grow the signature grape of Indiana, Traminette. Traminette is a hybrid grape producing an aromatic white wine with a body, color, and bouquet similar to a German-style wine such as Gewürztraminer.

The Muirs enjoy all aspects of owning a winery, but there are challenges, too. "We work seven days a week," explained David. "I would rather be outside, unless it's 95° and humid. Then I find something to do in the basement." The whole process though is fun and interesting to them. Taking the vines from bare sticks to a lush vineyard, picking and crushing the fruit, and creating wines people like is highly satisfying for them. Keeping the farm producing agricultural products was important also. "Opening the winery wasn't just for profit."

The Muirs are happy to provide a pleasant experience to all. "We are thankful for all of our friends and family who have helped our dream come true. We invite you to come visit us and taste the simple goodness Fruit Hills Winery has to offer." We heartily agree.

"The discovery of a wine is of greater moment than the discovery of a constellation. The universe is too full of stars."
– Benjamin Franklin

Fruit Hills Winery & Orchard
55503 State Road 15
Bristol, IN 46507
574-848-9463

Events: Yes, small events up to 30

Wine Trail: The Wineries of
   Indiana's Northeast Tour

Wines

Marquette
A cold, hardy hybrid that has Pinot Noir in its parentage, producing medium bodied red wine that is excellent with pasta, sausages and cheeseburgers.

Vignoles
A crisp, acidic white wine that pairs well with spicy dishes or pork dishes that are prepared with fruit glaze.

Make Me Blush
This wine is a blend of Concord and three white wines to create a well-balanced blend of sweetness and acidity. Serve with seafood in white sauces.

Red Sensation
A sensational sweet wine produced from a blend of hybrid red grapes. This wine is excellent with dark chocolate desserts.

Recipe

Apple Saucy

½ cup Fruit Hills Winery Apple Wine with Cherry juice

3 cups of chunky applesauce, plain or cinnamon

Directions:

Combine in saucepan and bring to a boil. Boil until slightly thickened, about three minutes, serve as a side dish. It's especially good with pork chops and fried potatoes.

GATEWAY CELLAR WINERY
GOSHEN

"I just want to make some good beer and good wine, have people enjoy it and have fun."
– Larry Libey

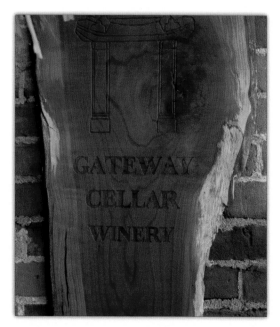

Whether owner Larry Libey is manning the bar in the brewery or serving wine in the winery, he has a booming voice with an interesting story to tell. One of them was about his first experience making wine. With some help from his father-in-law, he bought a can of grape juice concentrate and put it in a bottle. He decided to double the sugar and yeast that was recommended and put a balloon on top. He then set it in the basement to start the fermentation process. "I went down three days later to check on things and it looked like a geyser went off. There was no balloon to be found." Needless to say, his expertise in wine-making has gotten significantly better since then.

The winery first opened in 2006 and after being a customer of the first owner, Larry purchased the winery when it went up for sale in 2011. From the time he bought the winery, Libey had an eye toward opening a brewery, but that happened a bit quicker than expected when the back part of the building came up for sale. He opened the brewery in 2013. Both spaces are warm and inviting, with the traditional ceilings and structures of a building built in the 1880s.

"The building has housed many businesses," said employee Tami Cook. "It was a furniture store in the '60s, a general store at one time, and even a funeral home in the 1930s." Of course, the funeral home idea peaked our interest in ghost stories, and we found there's more than one kind of spirit hanging around at Gateway Cellar and events can happen at any time of the day or night. "We've had caps pop off bottles," Cook acknowledged. "Things will fall of

shelves and one employee reported that a roll of paper towels came flying off the shelf at him when he was here alone."

Cook was not the only one with a ghost story to tell. "The spirits here are mischievous," reported Libey. "A regular patron experienced a ghostly presence slip a hand inside his shirt and back out again." The look on his face said it all. Others have reported a silhouetted figure dressed in 1800s' style clothing. Despite all of this, don't be scared to come and join in all the fun at Gateway Cellar. "Make sure you tell them about the friendly atmosphere," suggested one of the patrons. That along with community involvement makes this winery a must stop.

The first Friday of each month, the whole town of Goshen celebrates. There's a theme and activities set up for all members of the family. "There are bands, food vendors, and some of the restaurants cook," …it's a big party. The businesses also decorate and participate. "There was a beach themed Friday one time," explained Cook. "The city brought in sand to make a volleyball court. Palm trees and flamingoes went up all over town." These events are very popular with people from inside and outside the city participating. "In the fall, a pottery maker comes in and sells bowls that are then filled with soup or chili. We have open mic every Thursday and bands on the first Friday and third Saturday of each month. There's always something happening for everyone at Gateway Cellar Winery.

Gateway Cellar Winery
211 South Main Street
Goshen, IN 46526
574-370-4049

Events: The wine bar is very popular to the area, offering live music and private parties. Call them for more information.

Wines

South African Pinotage Cabernet

Pinotage is a cross between Pinot Noir and Cabernet resulting in a full-bodied, complex wine with a velvety texture. Pair with hearty, thick stews.

Black Cherry Pinot Noir

Rich in complexity with a warm oaky flavor. Slight cherry nose with silky tannins. Pair with chocolate éclairs, pasta dishes that have both tomato and cream based sauces mixed together, and simple casseroles.

Pomegranate Zinfandel

This wine has a deep plum color with the sweet and tart flavor of pomegranate. Pack for the picnic basket or a girls' weekend.

Green Apple Gewurztraminer

This light and refreshing German-style wine is refreshing and light with hints of green apple. Pairs with Moroccan Cuisine, bacon, and dishes with cinnamon.

WHAT HAPPENS AT THE WINERY
STAYS AT THE WINERY

Recipe

Caramel Coffee Chill

1 cup Gateway Cellar Coffee Wine
Caramel Ice Cream Topping
Whipped topping
Strawberry garnish

Directions:

Pour coffee wine into shallow, metal pan, like a pie pan, and place in freezer. Allow to sit for about an hour or more until frozen (wine will not completely freeze.) Drizzle a small amount of ice cream topping into large wine glass. With a spoon, scrape wine into glass. Put a dollop of whipped topping on top, drizzle with ice cream topping, and garnish with a strawberry.

STONEY CREEK WINERY
MILLERSBURG

There's a very good reason that the outside of Stoney Creek Winery's tasting room looks like a gambrel roof barn; it is. "We started looking for a winery to purchase," explained Jeremy Plank. "But we couldn't find one so we cleaned out the barn and started building walls." The prairie-style barn was built in the 1950s and holds all the charm of that time updated with honeyed wood paneling and a unique tasting bar made of wine barrels with a fitted top. Owners Gary and Jan Plank, their sons Josh and Jeremy and Jeremy's wife Nickole have had the winery up and running since 2010, but it was quite a journey getting there.

Jeremy Plank took us back to when he was young to tell the winery's story. "We had a small farm here and there wasn't a lot to do." Being energetic kids, Jeremy and Josh looked for something to keep them occupied when farm work waned in the fall and winter.

"In the back of a seed catalog, we saw a wine making kit and asked Dad if we could order it. I was probably in middle school and Josh was younger." Their age didn't deter them from believing they could create a satisfying product, as wine making was a bit of a family heritage with four generations now having shared the tradition. "I remember my grandfather always making wine," said Jeremy.

The wine making kit arrived and Jeremy and Josh went right to work. "The concentrated grape juice came with the kit." They made their first batch and waited for it to be ready. "It was not good. I tried to add sugar, but didn't know I had to stabilize the wine." He and Josh had it in their bedroom. "At night, we could hear corks explode out of the bottle and hit the ceiling," Jeremy laughed.

The Plank brothers have come much further in their winemaking skills since then, producing several award-winning wines for Stoney Creek Winery, but their father Gary never tried his hand at it. "My wife Jan and I have two sons who have enjoyed making wine for many years and we have enjoyed drinking it," Gary chuckled.

"My dad never made wine," Jeremy explained. "But he and my mom used to visit wineries a lot. I kept suggesting we might want to open a winery, but it took a while to convince them." Gary finally decided to try to join them in the challenges of wine making and the staff at Purdue helped them all to see their dream of wine ownership through.

Finally, they were prepared and slated to open in 2009, but something intervened. On March 12, 2009, the family home burned down, which set them back for a year. Now the winery is a success and people visit from all over the United States and several countries.

"We try to make people as comfortable as possible so they can get the small winery experience," Jeremy said. This includes knowledgeable family members around to dispense tastings and share what they know about making wine, owning a winery, or just farm life in general. They invite all guests to come and experience their wines and the small farm winery lifestyle. Cheers!

Stoney Creek Winery
10315 C. R. 146
Millersburg, IN 46543
574-642-4454

Events: Yes, outdoor only,
up to 150

Wines

❧ Cabernet Sauvignon

This dry and mellow wine is often paired with hearty meatballs and spaghetti, game birds such as duck, and grilled steaks.

❧ Blanco

An off-dry, easy drinking and well-round fruity blend of Chardonnay, Muscat, and Riesling. Pair with chicken enchiladas covered in pepper jack cheese or crab cakes.

❧ Peach Apricot

Starts with a Chardonnay base then finishes in a perfect union of peach and apricot flavors. Splash over your favorite salad for a little pizzazz.

❧ Blackberry

Dark and fruity, this popular wine is locally grown and pure blackberry cobbler in a glass.

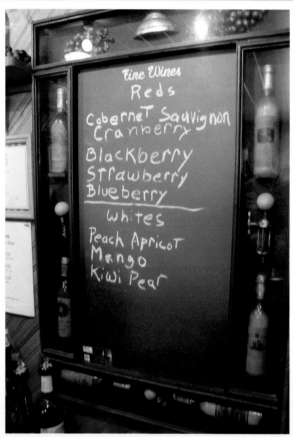

Pairing

We paired Stoney Creek's Cabernet Sauvignon with the recipe Red, White, and Yum! on page 31, (Shady Creek Winery) or pair with your favorite meatloaf or meatball sub.

BRIALI VINEYARDS & WINERY
FREMONT

The laid back atmosphere is so prevalent at Briali, it's hard to tell who are the workers and who are the visitors. When asked why Brian Moeller decided to open a winery, Brett Darrough quickly supplied, "He's insane."

Everyone laughed heartily, but totally understood the meaning. A winery with a full vineyard is not a light undertaking. Grapes can be a continuous cycle of pruning, training to grow on a wire system, keeping an eye out for pests and diseases, and hoping for a good harvest, all dependent on the weather and soil conditions. Then comes the harvest and making of the wine. With all of this, only one acre is a big undertaking. Looking at the beautiful vineyards stretching out over the ground at Briali, one can imagine the amount of work it took to get them to that point.

Briali Vineyards & Winery sits on the same property as Country Meadows Golf Course in Fremont, Indiana. They share a building and a parking lot, with the winery located in the lower part of the structure. Although the atmosphere is casual, owner Brian Moeller's dedication to bio-dynamic farming is not.

Biodynamic farming is similar to organic in the way the plants are approached with an all-natural form of gardening, but they do differ. Organic is emphasized by a whole approach towards the people, community, ecology, and working with existing organic systems.

On the other hand, a biodynamic farm is viewed as a single entity; an organism in and of itself with the soil seen as the central component of the farm. To that end, when Moeller first decided to plant his first acre of grapes, his first task was to get a soil sample.

"We found that after decades of commercial farming, the land was lacking food source for plants

Briali Winery
102 IN 120
Fremont, IN 46737
260-316-5156

Events: Yes, indoors up to 40;
outdoors up to 200

Trail: The Wineries of Indiana's
Northeast Tour

because of the use of chemicals. We planted clover and legumes that were tilled into the soil two years in a row. The purpose was to build soil structure and nutrients in what some people call a green fashion."

Getting the soil prepared was only the beginning of the journey, as grapes take a bit of babying to produce a lush harvest. The journey from the first spring planting until the first abundant grape harvest is about three years. Undeterred, Moeller was determined to build a vineyard based on biodynamic farming.

Some people may have heard about the waning number of honey bees, which are necessary for growing all types of fruits and vegetables due to pollination. However, many have also noticed a decline in earthworms, which help air and water get into the soil. They also break down things like leaves and grass and leave fertilizer. They are free farm help, and "not a scarce creature anymore, which is always a good sign. Briali's vineyard also draws large groups of bees and the rare Sphinx moth. "It's rare encounters like sphinx moths that keep us focused on keeping it green and striving to not damage our earth beyond the damage it has to battle already."

Moeller and his team's commitment to the vineyard and making good wine shines through in every well thought out glass. We suggest you visit soon and experience the clean taste of biodynamic farming.

Wines

◦ **Barbera**

This wine is light with a bite of fruit in your face. Pair with your favorite grill-out foods; steak, hamburgers, even hot-dogs.

◦ **Tempranillo**

This medium-bodied red wine finishes soft and smooth. It pairs well with a ham spiced with cloves and dark cherries, green beans, and mashed potatoes with butter and chives.

◦ **Blaufränkisch**

Dr. Frankenstein's bourbon barrel side project. Watch out y'all.

◦ **Geez**

The proper name for this white German-style wine is Geisenheim, but we can't say that. Pair it with a creamy macaroni and cheese, grilled chicken in white wine sauce, and spicy corn.

Recipe

Vignoles Breakfast Muffins

1 cup Briali Vineyards & Winery Vignoles wine, heated 30-45 seconds in the microwave

2 cups self-rising flour

1 egg

½ cup diced ham

½ cup shredded cheddar cheese

2 Tbls sugar

½ tsp garlic powder

1 stick of butter, melted

Spray oil

This is a great, easy, and tasty recipe. Set oven to 350°. Grease 12 cup muffin pan with spray oil and set in oven. Stir flour, sugar, and garlic powder together with wooden spoon. Mix in ham and eggs. Heat wine and add to flour mixture. Scrape sides to moisten all dry ingredients, and then mix until all dry ingredients are moistened. Pull muffin pan out of the oven and divide the dough evenly between the 12 muffin tins. Pour melted butter evenly on top. Bake for 25-35 minutes until golden. Let sit for five minutes and enjoy.

SATEK WINERY
FREMONT

"Good wine, good fun"
– Pam and Larry Satek

This year, Satek Winery celebrates their 16th year open to the public, but the grain of an idea to open a winery has been around a lot longer in the mind of Larry Satek. In 1975, while teaching at Washington College in Maryland, he and his wife rented a home in Chestertown, Maryland. There just happened to be grape vines in the backyard and Larry, a chemistry professor by trade, started playing around with wine making. Satek kept his wine making hobby even after moving to Illinois, before putting down roots in Indiana around 2001.

In 1992, Larry started planting and experimenting with his own grape varieties. Nine years later, he and his wife, Pam settled on a piece of property her great-grandfather purchased in 1915. The land is on the north end of Lake James near Kreibaum Bay. It had been a working apple orchard for many years, but became overgrown and had not been in commercial use for around 60 years when the Satek's first planted a vineyard.

The Satek's had decided to grow grapes for other vineyards, while keeping their regular jobs – Pam was a principal and Larry a research scientist. Their eye was always on opening their own winery, and they looked at the idea as a "retirement" plan. Many people see opening a winery as a romantic idea seen through rose colored glasses. The Sateks did their research and knew what they were getting into when they opened the winery in June of 2001.

Since opening, the winery has grown in leaps and bounds. When they first opened, it was only Larry, Pam, and one part-time employee. Now, there are

48

twenty-four employees. They began with only four types of wine and grew most of it themselves. The demand has been so great that they now keep about 30 wines at a time while experimenting with new and different flavors. Because of the more than 11,000 gallons of wine produced each year at Satek Winery, they've turned to local and other state vineyards to supplement the ones they grow.

In 2004, only three short years after opening, Satek earned the distinct honor of being named one of the top wineries in the state after winning twenty-one medals at the Indy International Wine Competition. This contest is the third largest in the United States. Satek Winery's DeChaunac, a signature dry red made from local grapes, won both a gold medal and a "Best in Class" award. Their Riesling also took home a gold medal that year. Since then, they've received many more accolades for their wines, including Wine of the Year for their 2008 Kreibaum Bay Vidal Blanc Ice Wine, and double gold for 101 Lakes White and their Blackberry Wine. Larry Satek stepped back a few years ago to take more of a consulting emeritus position. Shane Christ (rhymes with mist) is now the wine maker and has become part of the family, as well.

Larry's son, Jason, is also an integral part of the winery and seems to be everywhere he's needed at once. Although his job doesn't have a formal title, it could be Jack of all trades. A funny photo of him, with ice in his beard, hangs in the winery. Wine maker Christ showed off his photography skills and snapped it while they were picking frozen grapes to make ice wine.

The Satek's are very involved with the local community and love to host community events including Art Show at the Winery, Run N' Wine, and a Holiday Open House. Come and see the good folks at Satek's Winery soon, and bring your funny bone. The Sateks love to make people laugh.

Satek Winery
6208 N Van Guilder Road
Fremont, IN 46737
260-495-9463

Events: No

Trail: The Wineries of Indiana's Northeast Tour

Wines

❧ Whisper

Our popular dry white blend is a medley of pineapple and lemon. Crisp and fruit forward, pair with spicy Spanish or Indian dishes.

❧ Larry's Luscious Dry Red

Our award winning Meritage-style blend is composed of local and Indiana grown grapes. Spread goat cheese on slices of French bread and broil for a perfect complement to this wine.

❧ Soren's Favorite

Semi-dry white blend with hints of berries, spice and a Golden Muscat edge. It pairs well with gingered scallops or shellfish and peach desserts.

❧ Lakes White

Semi-sweet white blend with hints of apple and honeysuckle. Serve chilled with a fruit salad of cantaloupe, watermelon, and pineapple, or a flaky whitefish dinner.

Recipe

Mango-mosa
3 cups Satek Mango Mania Wine, chilled
3 cups fresh squeezed orange juice, chilled

Directions:
Pour the wine into a half-gallon pitcher and add orange juice. Stir and serve with an omelet and fruit salad. Perfect for a brunch or luncheon.

COUNTRY HERITAGE WINERY & VINEYARD
LaOTTO

*"It is our belief that great wine starts in the vineyard
or field with quality grapes and fruit."*
– Jeremy and Jennifer Lutter

Coming up the drive of Country Heritage Winery and Vineyards, visitors' mouths may drop open at the size of the winery and vineyards.

One acre of vines can produce between two and ten tons of grapes. One ton of grapes will produce about 720 bottles of wine. Country Heritage currently has 24 acres of grapes with plans to plant up to 100 acres. The sheer amount of wine they can produce on their property alone is mind boggling. But the building, with its huge gazebo and wrap-around deck is impressive too.

The farm where all of the winery magic happens has been in the Lutter family for over 100 years. Jeremy and Jennifer Lutter wanted to continue the agricultural heritage of their family and opened the winery on April 29, 2011. To ensure they created the best wine possible in their Northeast portion of Indiana, they hired friend and experienced vintner, Kevin Geeting.

"I researched the Marquette grape thoroughly," explained Geeting. "It grows well in Minnesota, and I thought it might be a good choice for our soil and weather. It also has one of the shortest growing seasons, so we had to be careful with the varieties we chose." Along with the grape wines, Geeting is not afraid to experiment with other fruits. "We made a pineapple wine that was very popular and sold out quickly. We'll make it again if I can find someone to

grow me pineapples," he laughed. His philosophy about the fruit they acquire for wines and ciders is a logical one.

"We get apples from a local grower, but we get cherries from Traverse, Michigan. If you can't grow it yourself, it makes sense to get it from the place where it grows best." He further explained, "We're still experimenting with fruit from all over and up and down the west coast. We want to show our versatility and have something for every customer who comes through the door." This they do to exception with their selection of dry to sweet and fruit wines, plus ciders. The building itself is also something guests often comment on.

The huge winery building is a feat of architecture. Jeremy Lutter is a farmer, by tradition, but is also a jack of all trades. "A big portion of the wood used in the winery came from Jeremy's own property and he built the bar, the wine racks, and all of the tables in the tasting room. His uncle built all of the doors," Geeting said with admiration in his voice. "He's a woodworker, winery owner, blueberry patch owner, and does almost any job around the farm that needs doing."

In addition to all of the building and farming, Jeremy and Jennifer are often behind the bar alongside their valued employees. They make the specialty fudge offered in the winery with exotic flavors such as peach-mango twist and lemon meringue, as well as traditional flavors of chocolate and peanut butter. The dark chocolate with black raspberry is heaven.

Touring the winery is not to be missed with a barrel of Chardonnay featuring a clear top. It's so clear you can clearly see a light shining at the back of the barrel. With all that Country Heritage Winery and Vineyard has to offer, including delicious wines, great hospitality, and live music and food trucks almost every Friday and Saturday night, once visitors come through the doors, they may find it very hard to leave.

Country Heritage Winery & Vineyard
0185 CR 68
LaOtto, IN 46763
260-637-2980

Events: Yes, corporate events and weekday rentals Monday-Thursday. Call for details.

Wines

⇾ Marquette
This Gold Medal winner is estate grown with notes of black currant and black cherries. Pair with a lamb or sausage dish generously mixed with mushrooms.

⇾ Vignoles
A Best in Class Double Gold Medal winner, the wine bursts with passion fruit and a zesty citrus flavor. Pair with a grill seared tenderloin, a salad filled with dried fruits and firm cheeses, or it makes a great marinade for a lemon pepper chicken dish.

⇾ Heritage Rose
This Silver Medal winner, a best seller, is a blend of Catawba and Concord grapes. An easy sipping and pairing wine; serve with any summer sandwich from chicken to fruit or even crab salad.

⇾ Black Raspberry
This Gold Medal winning dessert wine bursts with perfect sweet black raspberry flavors. Serve for dessert and pair with dark chocolate or pour over your favorite cake.

Recipe

Oh-La-Lobster Bisque

½ cup Country Heritage La Crescent wine
¼ cup cream sherry
1 ½ cups half and half
½ pound cooked lump lobster
¼ cup mushrooms, chopped
2 Tbs onion, chopped,
2 Tbs celery, chopped
2 Tbs carrots, chopped
14.5 oz clam juice
3 Tbs butter
⅛ tsp cayenne pepper
Salt to taste

Directions:

Melt butter in a large saucepan over medium-low heat. Add mushrooms, onion, celery, and carrots. Cook and stir until tender, about 10-15 minutes. Stir in clam juice and season with salt and cayenne pepper. Bring to a boil, turn heat down and simmer 10 minutes. Pour vegetable and clam mixture into blender or food processor, add ¼ cup of the lump lobster. Cover and process until smooth. Return to saucepan. Stir in the half and half, wine, sherry, and remaining lobster meat. Cook over low heat, stirring frequently, for thirty minutes. Bon Appétit!

TWO EE'S WINERY
HUNTINGTON

"Letting the Grape Speak"
– Eric and Emily Harris

The motto at Two EE's Winery, named for Emily and Eric Harris, "Letting the Grape Speak" comes from their belief that each variety of grape deserves a spotlight, because it has something unique to offer. After tasting the vibrant and individualistic flavors of the wines, we heartily agree.

While interviewing Dennis Hart, father of Emily and Operations Manager, it was clear that here was a man who enjoyed his work. "I get to work with my daughter and other family members. We're blessed to have an excellent staff that feels like family," he said. But it's not only the family aspect that inspires his ideal job. "I like the whole business," he exclaimed with a huge smile. "I'm an avid wine enthusiast. I like visiting wineries, making wine, and I love drinking it. I like the social aspect of it. I have a nice, diverse set of responsibilities."

Although Hart was happy to talk about his winery duties and interests, he was also quick to point out the accolades toward others at the winery. "My son-in-law and head winemaker, Eric Harris, was recognized in 2013 and 2014 as a Rising Star Winemaker." These awards were from the International Wine Channel, judged in Sonoma County, California. Eric has a wine making degree from UC Davis in California. "We made wine together so much after he and Emily began dating that we became very close friends right away," Hart said. In addition to Eric's talents, "Emily has a

degree in interior design from Indiana Purdue Fort Wayne. Since high school, she's worked part-time for a local interior design firm."

Emily used that knowledge to design a modern and sophisticated tasting room, where people feel comfortable and are able to relax. The back patio area is warm and inviting, with stone fire pits surrounded by tan wicker chairs. There are also remote control screens that block the wind, cold, and sun for maximum comfort. When the screens are closed, the fire pits and heaters make the patio a heated space for plenty of guests. The uncommon rock walls set up in front of and around the winery, are what's known as a gabion style. More common in the Western part of the US, this style consists of a wirework container filled with rock, or other materials and are often used in the construction of dams and retaining walls.

Two EE's Winery
6808 North US 24 E.
Huntington, IN 46750
260-672-2000

Events: Yes, small parties, bridal showers, charity events, etc.

The event coordinator for Two EE's Winery plans many music events featuring local talent and bands from as far away as Nashville and Pittsburgh. Fundraisers are often held at the winery, including a spring and fall 5K run through the 40-acre property. "It draws 400-500 participants each year."

Although they already have plenty on their plate, the people at Two EE's are always looking to the future. "We're thinking of adding an event space for weddings and large events," said Hart. "We've talked about larger vineyards, a brewery and maybe even a distillery."

Visit Two EE's Winery soon where they may have their eye toward the future, but their fully immersed in enjoyment of the present, and it shows in their customer service; and their wine.

Wines

❧ Barreja
This off-dry wine consists of three interesting blends. Very versatile and will pair well with curry and spicy dishes.

❧ Stuquette
This unique blend of Steuben and Marquette, is fruity and tantalizing. This easy sipping wine pairs well with fruit or vegetable salads, and meaty cheeseburgers.

❧ Grüner Veltliner
The spicy quality and bite of acidity will pair well with all types of food, but especially Asian cuisine. Seafood with ginger, turmeric, or other fragrant spices work well also.

❧ Plum
Starting sweet and finishing tart, this wine is a favorite for adding to a sangria, making a slushie, or it perfectly blends with red pasta sauces.

Pairing

Pair Two EE's Winery's Grüner Veltliner with the Ginger Scallops on page 138 (Chateau Thomas's recipe). This is a wonderful all-around wine to serve with spicy or savory chicken or seafood dishes.

MCCLURE'S ORCHARD & WINERY
PERU

"Living the Dream and Bottling it for You"
– Jason and Paige McClure

McClure's Orchard and Winery is an entire family experience with, among other things, a gift shop featuring jams and jellies, a petting zoo, The Apple Dumplin' Café, a pumpkin field, and, of course, apples to pick during harvest season. Visitors in the spring are treated to the sight of apple blossoms coming down like snow. One of the many highlights at the orchard is their wines and ciders. The owners of the farm, Jerry and Paige McClure, and their son and daughter-in-law, Jason and Alison McClure, have a simple philosophy for success: "We want to see production from our ground, to fruit, to bottle, then to the customer," explained Jason McClure. "Why not make a product that's local and more specifically, from our own farm."

He's very serious about getting all of the fruit used from their land. "We had a peach wine two years ago. Because of the weather, we haven't had peaches in two years, so no peach wine. People have asked us for a pear wine, so we've planted pear trees." They listen to their customers and are willing to experiment with different wines and ciders, which is only one aspect of their success. Jason and all of the McClure's aren't afraid to do whatever it takes to ensure the success of their orchard and winery. When asked to describe what his day had been like thus far on the day of the interview, the reply was exhausting.

"Today, Alison and I got up early, ate, and then fed a few calves and some other critters. I walked through the field with a rambunctious child and ran a disc over a pumpkin field." This was all before 10:00 am. "Later I'll finish the field, clean up the equipment and myself, then I'll be teaming up with the golf club to pour some wine and ciders for their open house." Jason

60

McClure's Orchard & Winery
5054 North US 31
Peru, IN 46970
765-985-9000

Events: Yes, indoor seating up to
80; outdoors, call for information

Wine Trail: The Wineries of
Indiana's Northeast Tour

thought he'd be home somewhere around ten that night, then up between five and six for the next day's chores.

Along with the apples, McClure's offers, when available, peaches,
pears, cherries, hops, pumpkins, gourds, red raspberries, black raspberries, blackberries, grapes, asparagus, and rhubarb, with plans to add
more. "But we don't want to outgrow the farm," Jason emphasized. "We
don't want to truck in fruit or juice to keep up with production." They
want to ensure that they know where the fruit comes from. In addition
to traditional wines and ciders, the McClure's offer some unique finds.

"We're the only winery to offer an ice cider." Similar to an ice wine,
this has been a very popular seller. "We freeze 300 gallons of juice. During thawing, the sugar will thaw first and that's what we use to make ice
ciders," Jason said.

When asked what she liked about working the farm, Alison stated,
"It's extremely challenging and extremely fun. There are good days and
bad days, but at the end of the day, it's very rewarding." We found our
experience very rewarding also and encourage you to visit McClure's
Orchard and Winery very soon.

Wines

❧ Apple

Made in dry, semi-sweet, and sweet varieties, this wine is smooth and crisp. Add the dry to chili or stew for an extra zing, and pair the sweet and semi-sweet with green salads with nuts and medium cheeses, blue, stilton, or sharp cheddar. They're great with fondues too.

parts rhubarb wine and balsamic vinegar, cook to reduce to half and it's a perfect sauce for pork loin or chops.

❧ Sweet Blueberry

Bursting with big fruit flavor, this wine pairs extremely well with duck, deer, and liver pâté.

❧ Steuben

A pretty blush, this wine is the perfect aperitif or pairs well with Asian spices or a chilled tuna or chicken salad.

❧ Sweet Rhubarb

Sweet up front and slightly tart on the finish, this wine pairs extremely well with strawberry desserts, cheesecake, or combine equal

From the Winery

Uncle Billy's Hard Cider
Soft Caramel Candies

1 cup McClure Orchard and Winery's Uncle Billy's
   Hard Cider
1 cup heavy cream
4 Tbl. unsalted butter
¼ tsp. sea salt
1 cup white sugar
¼ cup brown sugar
¼ cup light corn syrup
Candy thermometer

Directions:

Line bottom and sides of 8 x 8 dish with parchment paper. Boil Uncle Billy's Hard Cider until reduced by half, approximately 15 minutes on med-high heat, set aside. In a 4-quart saucepan over medium heat, melt butter and add cream. Add salt, sugars, corn syrup and hard cider reduction. Bring to a boil over med-high heat without stirring until the candy thermometer reaches 250 ° F. (Do not walk away from the pan at this point, as temperature control is very important to the texture of your caramels.) Remove from heat and pour into the parchment covered 8 x 8 pan. Let sit a minimum of 8 hours or overnight. With a sharp knife, cut into 1 x 1 inch squares and wrap in waxed paper. You can play with this recipe by adding different flavors of cider or wine. It's excellent with the coffee honey wine.

SCHNABELTIER ARTISAN CHEESE & WINE
ROCHESTER

*"All the good things. International Flavors. Local Ingredients.
All Made On Site In Rochester, Indiana."*
– Rex and Kris Robison and Matt Sutton

Guests who visit Schnabeltier will quickly notice the large platypus prominently displayed on their sign. A platypus is rare in the animal kingdom in that it's one of only a few egg laying mammals. According to their website, "Schnabeltier is the German word for platypus. The platypus has 'all the good things' from several animals-beaver tail for powerful swimming, a duck bill for scooping up food, webbed feet for propulsion, and not to mention those extremely poisonous spurs that give it a little bit of bad-assery." Here, you'll find "all the good things" the Midwest has to offer.

Schnabeltier is the only facility in the Midwest that focuses primarily on making cheese and wine. "Cheese with wine is very popular throughout Europe," explained vintner and cheese maker Glenn Goss. "Owners Rex and Kris Robinson saw wineries that made their own cheeses as they traveled the world and wanted to have that here." When the winery opened on Halloween, 2014, the owners, and wine and cheese makers could not have imagined what accolades awaited them within a short period of time.

At one of their first competitions, the 2015 Indy International Wine Competition, their Barr Lake Peach Apricot Chardonnay took both gold and best of class. The Black Cherry Pinot, Maxinkuckee Moscato, and Summit Pinot Gris all received silver, and the Millark Pinot Noir and Minnow Creek Riesling, took

bronze, respectively. In addition, for their first foray into the US Championship Cheese Contest in Madison Wisconsin, they brought home a gold medal, best of class, for their Chipotle Gouda. They first chose which wines to make by the palate development of the region, and they make cheeses to pair specifically with their wine selections.

"The palate in this area tends to be sweet, so we decided to focus on some sweets," explained Glenn. They've added a few others as they've grown.

"We're staying with traditional wines for now," said Haley Lehman, assistant wine and cheese maker.

Visitors have an easy time of choosing a wine to pair with selected cheeses, or vice versa, as both the cheese and wine labels suggest the best pairing of each. For example, the "Loyal Gouda" cheese proposes the Minnow Creek Riesling on the label and the Millark Pinot Noir recommends the Richland White Cheddar. The creamery can produce an astounding 500 pounds of cheese per day. "We specialize in flavored goudas," said Glenn. "We're also one of only three or four places in America that make a raclette," a semi-hard cow's milk cheese.

Schnabeltier Artisan Cheese & Wine
491 Apache Dr.
Rochester, IN 46975
574-224-3373

Events: Yes, Indoor seating up to 55; outdoors up to 270.

The cute tasting room is a mix of the products offered and fun decor. Several cow paintings adorn the walls and an open refrigerator with cheese takes up most of one wall. Ample, comfy sitting areas are available inside and out. Schnabeltier seems to always have one or more activities sure to hold the attention of any visitor. Wine glass painting, wine, cheese and canvas, knit and sip, Mother's Day pampering, and events for nearly every holiday on the calendar, just to name a few. Whatever you're looking for, from relaxing to active, Schnabeltier is sure to have something for everyone in your group.

Wines

Manitou Merlot

This dry wine explodes with hints of plums, black cherry, violets and orange citrus. Pair with spaghetti and meatballs, a spicy jambalaya, or Mediterranean spiced vegetables.

Summit Pinot Gris

This versatile semi-dry wine has a gentle floral scent with delectable spiciness and hints of citrus and almonds. Pair with salmon, sweet and spicy Asian foods, or even an order of fries.

Minnow Creek Riesling

This semi-sweet wine has vivid flavors of peach and apricot with a fresh, floral aroma. It pairs nicely with Latin or curry dishes.

Barr Lake Peach Apricot Chardonnay

This sweet wine has delicious peach and apricot flavors perfectly intermingled with hints of citrus. This wine is perfect to sip alone or pair with smoky meats, such as chicken or fish, and soft, mild cheeses, such as goat or brie.

From the Winery

Chardonnay Cheese Fondue

1 cup Nyona Chardonnay
8 oz. Schnabeltier Loyal Gouda
8 oz. Schnabeltier Gliss Gruyere
8 oz. Schnabeltier Rochester Raclette
2 Tbls. flour
¼ tsp. salt
¼ tsp. garlic powder

Directions:

Over double boiler or in a smaller saucepan over a larger saucepan filled with water, melt cheeses with wine on med-high heat. When almost melted, whisk in garlic, salt, and flour. Turn down heat and serve warm. It is not recommended to bring to a boil.

574-889-2509

"Fine Local Wines for Fine Local Tastes"
– Megan, Phil, and Dan McDonald

Before any buildings were built, the land Indian Trail Wines sits on had a big part in Indiana history. In much of the land settled in America, the first trails were animal trails. Native Americans would follow these while hunting and they became trails both the Native Americans and settlers used to guide them through territories. Next came dirt roads, which evolved into gravel and then paved streets. Before the final annexation of the state, where the tasting room sits was Native American territory. "You can still see the fence that separated the state from Native American territory," said Phil McDonald, one of the three owners of Indian Trail Wines. The others are Phil's sister-in-law Megan McDonald, and her son Dan McDonald.

The cornerstone from an early cabin also sits on the property and the name of the winery comes from the legend that Indians followed their usual trails, which crossed the porch of the cabin. Supposedly the Native Americans would often look into the windows, frightening the inhabitants.

This idyllic spot in north central Indiana sports a pond, gazebo, and wood cabin tasting room, which includes rustic furniture and a hand created bar. In the summer, bands play in the gazebo as patrons gather their chairs on the expansive lawn to share some music and camaraderie under the stars with the McDonald's as attentive hosts. The reasons the family decided to open a winery are varied and personal.

"Dan had been making wine since his college days at Penn State," explained Megan. "He moved back in 1996 and started making it as an amateur." Friend's approval of his wines spurred him to investigate mak-

Indian Trail Wines
7540 N CR 350 W
Royal Center, IN 46978
574-889-2509

Events: Yes, indoor up to 25;
    outdoor up to 100

ing it as a commercial vintner. "In 2006," Megan continued, "we put in 200 plants to see how they would do. There were 31 wineries at that time. We visited wineries, took some workshops, and learned a lot. When we opened in 2010, there were 55 wineries."

Phil grew up on the land, which was a former dairy farm. He insisted that wine making was a habit that got carried away. He shared a story and a chuckle about their first foray into planting the vineyard. "It was an especially wet spring that year. I lost a shoe and it's still out there somewhere."

One of Megan's reasons for going into the winery business is because of her father-in-law. He'd noticed that people who retired and sat around doing very little, don't seem to survive a long time after retirement. "He told me I should retire to something instead of only retiring from something."

The philosophy at Indian Trail Winery is community. "All of our grapes come from the Midwest and we have no imported juice," explained Megan. "We do a lot of things to stay involved with the local people. Bridal showers, reunions, car shows, graduations, and various charity events." A neighbor made the bent willow chairs and rockers set around the tasting room and Phil found some old tin ceiling tiles at an antique store. "I removed the old paint and rust," Phil said, "then painted them a copper color." Phil used these tiles to make a stunning tasting bar. Many of the work that needed to be done to create the homey winery, was accomplished by friends and family members. The McDonald's invite you to come anytime and share in their piece of country life, and their wines, any time.

Wines

❧ Prairie Sunset Red

This estate blend of two grapes creates a dry tasting sweet wine with earthy aromas and hints of spice. Pair with a pasta salad that includes pepperoni's and black olives or roasted potatoes mixed with olive oil and Italian spices.

❧ Homestead Red

A silver medal winner, this rich wine, thick with the taste of cherry, is our most popular estate grown wine to date. Definitely a wine for all occasions and with any meal.

❧ Plum Crazy

A smooth-bodied sweet red with a wide taste range, sweet to slightly tart, and a lasting finish. It works well with fruits, salads, and chocolate.

❧ Meadowlark White

Rich and sweet with notes of honey and made from our own grapes, this addition will surprise you with its soft strength and happy finish. Serve this versatile wine with a meat and cheese tray, sandwiches, or a plate of cookies.

From the Winery

Settlers Pride Turkey Casserole (serves 8)

It's a great way to use left over Thanksgiving Turkey

½ cup Settlers Pride Rose Wine (a semi dry Catawba wine)

8 oz. spaghetti, macaroni, or noodles 6 Tbs. butter (¾ stick)

8 oz. mushrooms, sliced (2 ½ cups) ½ cup all-purpose flour

1 ½ cup chicken broth 1 ½ cup milk or half and half

4 cups chopped and cooked Turkey ½ cup Slivered Almonds, toasted

½ cup grated Parmesan cheese

Cook the pasta in boiling water. While pasta is cooking, melt butter in a large sauce pan. Add mushrooms to butter and cook until soft (about 5 minutes). Stir in until well blended ½ cup flour. Slowly add broth, wine and milk while whisking. Bring to a boil, reduce heat and cook until sauce is thick and smooth (about 5 minutes). Add turkey, almonds and pasta. Pour into a 13x9 baking dish and top with Parmesan cheese. Bake at 350 degrees until the sauce is bubbly and cheese is golden brown (about 30 minutes).

THE PEOPLE'S WINERY
LOGANSPORT

When you work in a building that's over one hundred years old, you're likely to hear noises now and then, but most can be explained. However, others defy explanation.

"We had a party here one evening," said tasting room manager Amy Schroder. "After everything was cleaned up and I was the only person in the building, I turned off all the lights and sat in the corner relaxing with a glass of wine. The only light came from the street lamp outside. I heard someone walking across the floor upstairs and the sound of glass breaking." Thinking another employee might have still been upstairs, she turned on the lights and went to check it out. "There was no one there, no broken glass, nothing. If there are ghosts, they're friendly and seem happy to have the building occupied again," Schroder added.

The People's Winery is housed in a building that was originally The People's Bank. The building was saved by the Historic Landmark Foundation of Indiana and it's on the historic register. Boarded up for over 35 years, the owners, Stacie and Brad Angle, bought the building and completely refurbished it, opening it as a winery in the spring of 2011.

"They took down some of the interior brick walls and used those to build the tasting bar," Schroder explained. In addition, the owners used rich

colors to highlight the walls and set off some local artists' work, giving it an elegant, relaxed feel. Some regular patrons have gifted them some of the wall coverings including an intricately decorated guitar and a metal print of the building's exterior. The atmosphere at The People's Winery, naturally draws visitors to the lovely space.

"We have people that bring in food, buy a bottle of wine and enjoy," said Schroder. "We have one group that brings in board games every week." When they have musicians come in to play, it's usually a packed house. The winery has become a neighborhood gathering spot, and that's just the way the owners like it.

Along with their ghostly spirits, The People's Winery offers an array of tasty wines suitable for every palate. These include a large array of interesting dry wines, and a caramel port-style wine. Everything is made in small batches to ensure quality and each bottle is labeled and bottled by hand. Whether your visit is prompted by camaraderie, liquid spirits, or the other kind, you'll find everything you're looking for at The People's Winery.

Q: What culture is thought to have begun making wine?
A: Mesopotamia (ancient Greece) is thought to have been the cradle of the beginning of wine making about 6,000 BCE.

The People's Winery
414 South Third St.
Logansport, IN 47947
574-721-0791

Events: Yes, indoor seating only, up to 50.

Wines

❧ Amarone

Rich raspberry, blackberry, and intense dark currant flavors, plus a deep, dark, and long-lingering finish full of ripe tannins. This dry red wine pairs well with salami pizza, your favorite pot roast, or grilled steaks with herb butter.

❧ Rosso Grande

Deep ruby-garnet color and intense with spicy oak aromas, this dry wine carries the vibrant flavors of ripe berry and black cherry. It pairs with the same foods as Amarone.

❧ Gewürztraminer

Aromatic and rich with the character of tropical fruit, this semi-dry white is a perfect match for spicy foods.

❧ Fuzzy Passion

The luscious scent of ripe peach is exceptional in this crisp flavorful wine. A natural addition to a lazy afternoon or picnic with soft cheeses, spicy ham, and buttery crackers.

Pairing

Pair The People's Winery's Amarone with your favorite lasagna recipe, or use our favorite from page
125. (Tonne Winery)

The Central Region

TJ HAASE WINERY • *Clinton, Vermillion County*
WINDY RIDGE VINEYARD AND WINERY • *Cayuga, Vermillion County*
COAL CREEK CELLARS • *Crawfordsville, Montgomery County*
BLACKHAWK WINERY AND VINEYARD • *Sheridan, Hamilton County*
HOPWOOD CELLARS WINERY • *Zionsville, Boone County*
TRADERS POINT WINERY • *Indianapolis, Marion County*
EASLEY WINERY • *Indianapolis, Marion County*
HARMONY WINERY • *Fishers, Hamilton County*
COUNTRY MOON WINERY • *Nobelsville, Hamilton County*
MADISON COUNTY WINERY • *Markleville, Madison County*
BELGIAN HORSE WINERY • *Middletown, Henry County*
TONNE WINERY • *Muncie, Delaware County*
J & J WINERY & NOBLE ORDER BREWING COMPANY • *Richmond, Wayne County*
BUCK CREEK WINERY • *Indianapolis, Marion County*
MALLOW RUN WINERY • *Bargersville, Johnson County*
CHATEAU THOMAS WINERY • *Plainfield, Hendricks County*

Additional Wineries
(see page 294 for information)

ASH AND ELM CIDER CO. • *317-250-3386 (Back of Book)*
CHATEAU DE PIQUE INDIANAPOLIS TASTING ROOM • *317-578-7413*
DANIEL'S VINEYARD • *877-994-7273 (Back of Book)*
NEW DAY CRAFT • *888-632-3379 (Back of Book)*
PEACE WATER WINERY • *317-810-1330 (Back of Book)*
WILSON WINES • *765-853-5100 (Back of Book)*

TJ HAASE WINERY
CLINTON

"Uncork and Re-wine!"
– Doug and Cathy Haase

When Doug Haase was young, he thoroughly enjoyed helping an Italian lady grind grapes and stir the barrel while she made wine. "Botcha," boy in Italian, is what she called him and the wine with this name is in her honor. This sweet lady inspired him to try his hand at winemaking. What kept him reaching for a winery dream was the Italian heritage of his mother. He wanted to emulate the Italian way of serving wine to everyone who lives within the community. For people who have visited Italy or immersed themselves in Italian culture, they learn that their way of slowing the pace leads to a less stressful lifestyle. The Haase's have lived in Clinton, Indiana their entire lives and are trying to bring a small bit of Italy into their community.

After starting their winery journey, the Haases visited many wineries to get a feel for what it took to own and run a winery. They traveled to many wineries throughout the country, taking things from each they liked and adding their own special touches. They especially like the wineries in the famed Finger Lakes region of New York, where they gained quite a bit of knowledge. They brought all they learned back to Clinton and on November 8, 2014, sponsored a food and wine tasting to introduce people to their new venture.

TJ Haase Winery
708 East 3rd Street
Clinton, IN 47842
812-241-9463

Events: Yes, both indoor and
outdoor; call for details

Visitors who follow the Indiana limestone path that leads to the quaint tasting cottage get the full small home-farm winery experience. The customer service is beyond compare, with someone greeting all who come through the door. The cute, rustic style interior includes comfortable seating areas, checked tablecloths, and checkerboards for guests who wish to play a game or two. A split-rail fence separates the tasting bar from the rest of the room.

A sense of fun exudes from this winery and one place it is found is in the cute wine labels, designed by Cathy Haase, and the stories that go along with some of the names of the wines. Shelbi Rigsby, a friend of the family who was tending the wine bar the day we visited, told the tale of The Drunk Donkey, a refreshing blackberry wine. "After fermentation, we often scoop out the leftover fruit, take it to Cathy's father's farm, and sprinkle it over the donkeys' feed. One batch turned out to be stronger than they realized," Shelbi laughed, "and Floyd, the donkey, charged through the electric fence and made his escape. They tried to get him back into the pen, with no luck. They had to call the sheriff's office to help corral him and get him back into the pen."

The Haases make all of their wines on the premises and have kept this tradition of naming wines, and even the winery, around things important in their lives. The TJ in TJ Haase Winery are the initials of Doug's son Tyler Jacob, who sadly passed away in 2010. "We opened this winery to keep his memory alive and keep our actual dreams alive also," they said. First to Dance, a Pinot Grigio, is the first wine they ever bottled in the production room called, "Tyler's Cellar." Pink Houses is a nod to the singer John Mellencamp, who grew up nearby and Hoot Owl is in remembrance of a very dear friend, Linda, who loved owls. This kindness toward everyone can be felt whenever visiting.

Locals come to share their music on the stage they built, named "The Shady Stage." People bring their chairs, buy a bottle of wine, and enjoy the music under the stars. They make the facility available for birthday parties, bridal showers, baby showers, and weddings. They also sell salami/cheese/cracker combos or you can feel free to carry in your own snacks or order up a pizza and have it delivered. It's a family friendly atmosphere where everyone is welcomed, even those under twenty-one. "We want customers to come in and relax, forget about the stress, and enjoy yourself." Come and soak in the warmth, friendship, and wine at TJ Haase soon. You'll be back.

Note: Photographs for TJ Hasse Winery were provided by Kathy Woodhouse.

Wines

Pink Houses

This Sauvignon Blanc's name comes from the song of famous Indiana singer John (Cougar) Mellencamp. It pairs well with vegetables, rice dishes, and light, flaky fishes.

Italian Stallion

A Sangiovese wine, this one knocks you out with its flavors. Pair with cured meats, hard cheeses, and starchy dishes.

Hoot Owl

Honoring a good friend, and owl lover, who passed away from breast cancer, this blueberry wine is a sweet treat.

Mixed Emotions

Containing both strawberry and banana flavors, this wine is the one to pack for a girlfriend's weekend.

From the Winery

TJ Haase Milani Crock Pot Roast

2 cups Milani (or a good dry red)
½ cup brown sugar
3 cups ketchup
1 large or 2 small chuck roasts

Place roast in crock pot and season with salt and pepper. Mix wine, brown sugar and ketchup in a bowl then pour over the roast. Cook on low for eight hours. The juice can be drizzled over the meat before eating. I also like to pair the roast with Brussel sprouts. I cut the Brussel sprouts in half and sauté them in butter.

WINDY RIDGE VINEYARD & WINERY
CAYUGA

"We take pride in growing and processing our grapes from vine to wine and shine."
— The McLain Clan

On the day we visited this winery, it certainly lived up to its name. The winery sits on the highest point in Vermillion County, Indiana. It's windy all the time, but it was especially strong on the day we were there. We giggled as we fought the wind to get the door open. To say the least, it wasn't a good hair day. However, the warmth and friendship we felt once inside was beyond compare.

Windy Ridge is a family owned and operated winery, distillery, and vineyard. They also make delicious wood fired brick-oven pizzas. The winery tasting room, which opened in August of 2012, has a hunter's cabin feel with animal heads and various game birds on the walls. There is a lot of good na-tured teasing that takes place between the members of this family-owned winery and their guests. "This was not the plan," patriarch Russell McLain ex-plained. "We wanted to plant a few vines, just to see if they would grow and we could make a little wine. We would have never been here if not for Justin's passion," he said.

Justin is Russell and Vicki's son, who began mak-ing wine as a hobby. He found he liked the technical aspects of trying to create perfect wines. "My wife Linda and I started to go to wineries," Justin said. They traveled as far as a Southwest Michigan wine trail. "After checking into it, I asked Dad to reduce his cattle herd to plant an acre of grapes."

"I said," laughed Russell, "if we're going to plant one, we might as well plant two. We wanted to plant a few grapes, just to see if we could make a little wine." Windy Ridge now has six acres of grapes. The "we" Russell spoke of also includes Justin's brother Jason and his wife Angie. When their first grapes came in, about a half a ton's worth, they made wine in five gallon buckets so they could experiment with it.

"We blended and messed with it," explained Justin. "Boiled sugar, which we really didn't need to do, and just piddled and kept messing with it until we came up with Pass the Buck and Desperado, which became the biggest sellers." They let friends and family taste the wine and were told it was good enough to sell. They've advanced from the five gallon buckets now and have stainless steel tanks and more sophisticated equipment. Even with parts of it being easier, the amount of work it takes to maintain the vineyards and make wine, plus run the winery, is enormous. "The vineyards are so much work," said Justin. "Picking, mowing, pruning, and spraying, we need help to get it all done. We didn't even know there were grape picking machines until last year," he laughed. In order to be allowed to spray the vines, Justin had to learn how to apply the spray and test for an applicator's license from Purdue. Justin described his title as "wine guru, fermenter, distiller, and sprayer." His dad Russell is the "foreman, grape picker, and delivery man." His brother, Jason, would be known as the "groundskeeper, sales guy, and runner." All the men and their wives help out in the winery.

Since they regularly have several thousand gallons of bulk wine, the McLains decided to pull some of that down by making brandy, moonshine, and other spirits. This adds yet another layer to what is so special about Windy Ridge Vineyard and Winery. The bottles they use for this are reminiscent of what moonshine might have been sold in during the bootlegging period of Prohibition. We invite you to visit the McLains at Windy Ridge very soon. Afterwards, you'll find yourself daydreaming about when you'll be able to make the next trip back. Cheers!

Note: Photographs for Windy Ridge were provided by Kathy Woodhouse.

Windy Ridge Vineyard
  & Winery
3998 N 150 W
Cayuga, IN 47928
765-492-9550

Events: Yes, in the summer mont

Wines

❧ Wooly Bully

A dry red wine made from a blend of Buffalo and Marechal Foch grapes, this pairs well with lasagna, Italian spiced dishes, or a piece of dark chocolate.

❧ Running Bear

This fruity wine has hints of elderberry, black currant, and black cherry. It pairs with roasted meats and vegetables and starchy side dishes.

❧ Blue on Black

A blueberry and blackberry sweet blend, this is a perfect sweet wine for sipping. Another idea is to bring a cup to a boil, allow to cool, and mix in powdered sugar ¼ cup at a time until thickened. Use as a topping for ice cream, cheesecake, pie, or cake.

❧ Paw-Paw

A sweet white made from Indiana Paw-paws, this wine is the one you want while sitting on the back porch watching the sun go down.

Recipe

French Onion Soup

1 cup Windy Ridge Vineyard and Winery Wooly Bully
   wine
French bread sliced and toasted
3 medium sized onions, sliced, not diced
2 cloves garlic, minced
1 stick of butter
32 oz. beef broth
2 beef bouillon cubes
2 tbsps. Worcestershire sauce
Pinch of ground cayenne pepper
Swiss cheese slices
Salt and pepper to taste

Directions:

Sauté onions and garlic with the butter in a large saucepan until onions are translucent. Add wine and cook for 3-5 minutes. Then add the bouillon cubes, broth, Worcestershire sauce, cayenne pepper, salt and pepper and simmer for 30 minutes. Toast slices of the French loaf of bread. Fill small soup crocks ⅔ full with the soup, add a slice of the French bread toast, then two slices of Swiss cheese. Broil in the oven until the Swiss cheese is bubbly and starting to brown. Serve hot. Bon appetite!!

COAL CREEK CELLARS
CRAWFORDSVILLE

Although we arrived on a cold winter's day, the cherry red barn tasting room gave us a warm feeling and the hearty greeting we received inside, furthered the glow. A fire burned in the fireplace and the cozy décor made everyone feel at home. Since it was a chocolate weekend, there were selections of delectable candies to sample. A pinball machine sat nearby and we were overcome with nostalgia as we played a few games, trying to beat each other's scores. The barn wood tasting bar gives an old time feel to the refurbished barn that is over one hundred years old. Everything about Coal Creek Cellars was designed with the customer in mind.

They offer fifteen varieties of wine to satisfy any wine palate from dry to sweet. They have chosen to make wines from traditional grapes such as Chambourcin, Norton, Riesling, and Vignoles. The picturesque view from the decks is the perfect spot to share a bottle of their impressive wines, which all carry excellent body, color, and flavor. Situated just west of Crawfordsville, this unique winery has a lot of interesting stories to tell.

Partner Chiral Waterman began her journey toward wine because her grandmother owned a winery. "I helped her out a lot, working in her vineyard." She made fruit, berry, and other types of wine in the San Joaquin Valley of California, where she grew up. "I

said I'd never work in a vineyard again." Since California is often seen as the quintessential place for American wine, people ask all the time, "You're from California? Why would you move here?" "From the first time I saw this area, I loved it. There was no going back."

Owner Ron Wojtaszek began when he met Thomas Coyne in California looking for volunteers to help in the wine making process. Along the way, he learned to make wine. Thomas Coyne, (1940-2015) was a famed winemaker in the Livermore Valley, California wine community. With a passion and knowl-

edge of what it takes for the sun and magic to turn fruit into wine, he made himself available to home and professional winemakers alike. He was well loved and admired and colleagues laughed over his ever-present Penn State ball cap and his parking spot for Penn State alums. With Coyne's help, Wojtaszek's winemaking skills and love for the whole process grew. (*Independent News*, July 2, 2015.)

The barn on the property is over 100 years old. When Wojtaszek bought the property, he wanted to preserve the agricultural ways the area is known for, but also wanted to update. They hired a local construction company to remake the barn into a tasting room. They kept the original timbers and repurposed windows and other things from different buildings to create a space that welcomes all members of the family, as it's designed to make visitors feel as if they are at home. Duck decoys sit around the room as homage to a family member who collects them and loves to hunt.

Local artists work adorns walls and fills space in the small gift shop. Stained glass pieces add a touch of elegance here and there. The winery designs and decorates gift baskets that are customized to the customers' wants and needs. Whatever your wishes are with wines, decorations, baskets, or fun, the people at Coal Creek Cellars can make them come true.

Note: Photographs for Coal Creek Cellars were provided by Kathy Woodhouse.

Coal Creek Cellars
3573 West U.S. Highway 136
Crawfordsville, IN 47933
765-362-3634

Events: Yes, call for details

Wines

Petite Sirah

A full-bodied dry red wine with tastes of blackberry and pepper. Great with an herbed encrusted whitefish, turkey, or sharp cheddar cheese.

Harmony

This fruity blend of four reds is aged in oak. Pair it with pizza, ham sandwiches, and slow cooked pork or lamb stews.

Cayuga White

Produced in dry, off-dry, and semi-sweet varieties, this versatile wine suits most palates. Great served with light foods.

Sweet Serenity

This port-like wine is slightly sweet and fortified. Serve before dinner or with a favorite sweet chocolate or berry dessert.

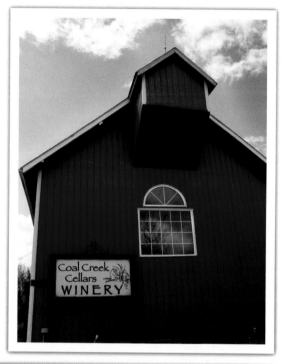

Recipe

Summer Refresher

1 bottle Coal Creek Cellars Riesling, chilled
1 large orange, sliced thin
1 small cucumber, peeled and sliced thin

    Mix all ingredients together in large pitcher. Refrigerate until needed. Serve when friends drop by on a hot day, at a garden party, or even at a sundown party.

BLACKHAWK WINERY & VINEYARD
SHERIDAN

"Wine is simply meant to be enjoyed. Period."
– John and Deb Miller

When pulling into Blackhawk Winery and Vineyard, visitors are often greeted by a small horse named Kirby. Actually, it's a large dog breed known as an English Mastiff. Kirby is but one of a menagerie of animals that include chickens, ducks, baby doll sheep, horses, and cows that are all a part of what gives Blackhawk its charm. The tiny baby doll sheep are so cute guests have to touch them to see how soft their wool is. One of the driving factors to owning so many pets is part owner Deb Miller, who is a veterinarian. She is also involved in the winery in a most important way. "Her main

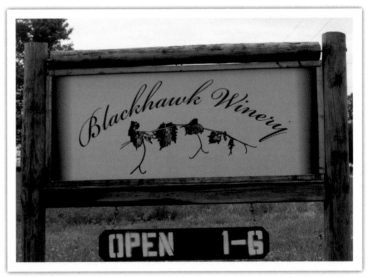

title at the winery is Official Wine Taster," joked her husband and other winery owner, John Miller. "It's a tough job, but someone has to do it." Along with the Millers, their son, Scott Miller and family friend, Avery Finchum, help out. They described their job title as "everything that needs to be done."

John calls himself a "recovering electrical engineer." He worked in the semi-conductor industry and if you've used an Intel CPU in a computer, John was probably involved somewhat in the manufacturing process. He'd been making wine as a hobby for years, starting with

kits and juice and eventually expanding to grapes until now he is Blackhawk Winery's winemaker.

When choosing which types of grapes to grow in their 8 acre vineyard, so many factors go into the process. Central Indiana, where Blackhawk Winery and Vineyard is located, experiences a variety of temperatures, sometimes all within the same week. Winter lows can get well below freezing. Ice and snow are the norm, but winter days can be in the '40s and '50s at times. Early spring frosts can seriously affect the emerging buds, and wet, humid summers can set

them up for many diseases. The Millers chose the varieties of grapes they planted with help from Purdue's Wine Grape Action Team. The people heading this team are enology professor, Christian Butzke, viticulture professor, Bruce Bordelon, and enology specialist, Jill Blume.

A viticulturist is an expert in scientific studies of grapes and their production for wine. Other foods and beverages can be studied by a viticulturist, but the main focus is wine. An enologist is a scientist who studies the chemistry and biology of wine. They assess the needs of the winery in relation to the wine and help them to produce the best wine possible.

The Millers chose both American and French-American hybrid vines for their winery. Their wines include the traditional Traminette, and the not so traditional Leon Millot and Sheridan, along with eight other varietals. Blackhawk Winery and Vineyards offers a variety of wines from dry to sweet and some port-style wines.

The Millers are serious about their wines, but they're also serious about being a part of their community. They sponsor a lot of community fundraisers and one dollar from every bottle of Blackhawk Rosé wine goes to support a music program at a local school. In addition, they hold a community Easter egg hunt, strawberry festival, and birthday celebration each year. They offer painting and craft classes throughout the year and have music every Friday and Saturday in the summer. Whether you're looking to sit back and relax with a few friends and a bottle of wine, or join in with some of the many activities, Blackhawk Winery and Vineyard is your one stop shop.

Wines

❧ Marechal Foch

Dry and fruit forward with a hint of spice on the finish, this wine pairs well with hearty soups like vegetable beef or starchy dishes like mashed potatoes with brown gravy.

❧ Prairie Red

A semi-sweet wine with hints of berry flavors and aromas of black cherries, it pairs well with a tuna steak sprinkled with lemon pepper or roasted and smashed cauliflower.

❧ Razzy Yuga

This blend of raspberry and Cayuga wines is perfection in a glass. Neither too sweet nor too tart, it highlights the flavors of soft cheeses, such as goat or gruyere, as well as light desserts like strawberry shortcake.

❧ Firefly (sparkling wine)

This bubbly and sparkling sweet white wine pops on your tongue with a crisp blend of citrus and apple flavors. Pair it with a light, flaky fish, buttered vegetables, and your favorite crusty bread.

Recipe

Tipsy Tacos

Although this recipe sounds simple, it's unbelievably delicious.

About 2 cups Blackhawk Winery Marechal Foch
1 taco or burrito kit
1 pound ground beef
1 small onion, diced
1 medium red pepper, diced
Shredded lettuce
Shredded sharp cheddar cheese
Sour cream

Directions:

In medium skillet, put onion and pepper over medium-high heat and pour enough wine in to almost cover them. Let cook until them cook, stirring occasionally, until all the liquid has been absorbed and vegetables start to brown; about twenty minutes. While the onion and pepper are cooking, brown ground beef in large skillet and drain. When the onion and pepper are finished, add them to the ground beef. Mix in taco or burrito seasoning packet and ¾ cup of wine. Heat through and serve with taco or burrito shells, lettuce, cheese, and sour cream.

Tip: To keep all the fillings from falling out of your tacos, mix sour cream into lettuce and cheese so they all stick together.

HOPWOOD CELLARS WINERY
ZIONSVILLE

"We Focus on Creating the Most Awesome Wines Possible."
– Ron Hopwood

It's hard to describe the atmosphere at Hopwood Cellars in just a few words. It's reminiscent of an elegant parlor with a European feel. The lovely accent of Simone Bednarek, the tasting room manager and event coordinator, extends that impression even further.

The board games, chess set, and comfy seating area give the atmosphere of a family room and when owner and wine maker Ron Hopwood is the one pouring wine tastings, his quick wit and warm personality make people feel as if they're at a neighborhood hangout. Whichever way visitors describe the winery, they will all agree on one word. Magnificent!

Hopwood Cellars Winery sits in the heart of the village of Zionsville. Guests feel as if they've stepped into a rift in time when visiting this quaint town. The streets are brick pavers. There's plenty of free parking and local restaurants and shops fill the buildings. Everyone stops to talk and share news around the town square.

Ron Hopwood explained his journey to becoming a winery owner very simply and succinctly. "It's a hobby gone wild. I started making wine in the basement and it grew from there." Wearing a lab coat, he looked very much like the chemist that all wine makers must become in order to make really

94

good wines. Creating good wine is only one aspect of having a successful winery and Hopwood cuts no corners here. "What sets us apart is excellent customer service. I hire the right people. It took me three years to find Simone. She is the liaison between the customer and the wine."

Watching Simone work, we could see why she was the perfect fit at Hopwood Cellars where she deftly poured wine and prepared food, while chatting with customers, putting them at ease. She seemed to be all over the room at once.

Hopwood is not afraid to try new things with both the food and wine at the winery. Ron serves an edible wild hibiscus flower soaked in a special raspberry and rhubarb sauce as well as bread with dipping oil, meats, and specialty cheeses. In the summer, they serve a wine shake that has become very popular.

When deciding on what wines to make, Hopwood studied the area in which he planned to open the winery. "Zionsville is a dry red town. I kept seeing the same four wines when there are over 5,000 types of wine grapes. I wanted to introduce new wines and experiences to the people who come through the doors." He currently has eight dry wines with plans to make more. Although he loves the dry wines, Hopwood also enjoys the sweets. "When I have a peanut butter and jelly sandwich, I reach for Sweet Lailah," a light flavored concord.

Hopwood Cellars is a gathering place for the locals and visitors who might wander through their doors. It easily becomes one group of people with like minds about good food, wonderful conversation, and great wines. Cheers!

Hopwood Cellars Winery
12 E. Cedar Street
Zionsville, IN 46077
317-873-4099

Events: Yes, indoor only, seating for up to 49.

Trail: Cardinal Flight Wine Trail

Wines

❧ Frontenac

A beautiful garnet color and distinctive cherry and lavender aroma wine, it is lightly oaked and robust. Pair with steaks and other beef dishes.

❧ Sunbaked Mihr

This wine, made with Marechal Foch grapes, mingles the taste of berries and plum. It works well with meatballs and spaghetti, lasagna, any red pasta sauce dish.

❧ Kabinette

This dry wine picks up light flavors of peach, pineapple, and nectarine. It's very versatile and pairs with many foods including Fettuccine Alfredo with chicken or ham, fresh or roasted vegetables, and a meat and cheese plate.

❧ Chambourcin Rosé

Raspberry aromas lead to notes of cherry and strawberry juiciness on the tongue. This is the wine to serve at an outdoor picnic or barbecue. Works well with everything from a pasta salad to a sirloin steak.

From the Winery

Hopwood Cellars Dipping Oil

One cup of olive oil
½ Tbl. Dried Rosemary
½ Tbl. Dried Thyme
¾ tsp. Paprika

Combine all ingredients and let them sit for a while to develop the flavor. Serve with bread for dipping. Pair with Hopwood Cellars Cabernet Sauvignon. You can add some wine to the dipping oil to enhance the taste.

TRADERS POINT WINERY
INDIANAPOLIS

As America was first being settled, rivers were often the most efficient way to transport goods and people from one place to another. Because of this, ports sprang up along oceans and rivers in the most convenient places according to population. Traders Point is a small town in Marion County where Lafayette road crosses over Eagle Creek. It's the first settlement in this part of Indiana and it's believed the first settlers made roads following Native American trails. This is what led to the beginnings of the city often filled with fur traders and others making business transactions. Bill Durr, part owner of Traders Point Winery along with his wife Lisa, named the winery because of his interest in history and as a nod to remember the beginnings of the area.

When a grist mill was established, the town saw more residents move close by. A grist mill is a large circular stone wheel, turned by a water paddle, which pounded grains such as wheat and corn into flour and meal in order to use in cooking. The animal and Native American paths, cities on rivers, and grist mills led to the settlement of America's large cities.

For Bill Durr, his winery path began many years ago. Curious about making wine, he began experimenting in the root cellar of his home in historic New Augusta. This was in the 1990s with home kits. "I made some dandelion wine that turned out well. The kids saw me picking the dandelions and asked if they could help. It was the Tom Sawyer effect," Bill laughed. He's referring to Tom Sawyer's feat of convincing his friends to whitewash his Aunt Polly's fence because they were missing out on the fun.

Traders Point Winery
5520 West 84th Street
Indianapolis, IN 46268
317-879-9463

Events: Yes, indoor only, up to

Trail: Cardinal Flight Wine Tra

After using different fruits and juices for his experimentations, Bill and Lisa decided to enter some wine into the amateur category at the Indy International Wine Competition. His wines did very well and this was the first time the idea of opening a winery started. During vacations, they would visit wineries throughout Indiana and other states. They also worked at a winery so they could learn the business from the ground up. The Durrs decided they wanted to experience the winery lifestyle and chose the name before starting the licensing process. Bill was the main driver behind the winery idea.

"I'm just here for the wine," joked Lisa. "It got too expensive to visit wineries." The Durrs children, Eric and Leah, designed all the labels. After years of research and more wine experimentation, the Durrs opened Traders Point Winery in November of 2013.

They decide what wines to make based on peoples' tastes. They try different ones and keep what sells well. Bill is not afraid to try different blends that you won't find at a lot of wineries, including a blackberry and cherry blend called Midnight Cherise. It's a best seller, along with Strawberry Shortcake. The unique names of their wines reflect both people in their lives and their sense of fun. Surr-N-Durr is a play on their name and Purdy Good, a white wine blend, is named after a family they've known for years. We highly recommend the Paradise Peach when you visit; it's like biting into a piece of summer.

Although it's taken years of hard work to get to the point where the Durrs could open the winery, they wouldn't trade the experience. We suggest you come to Traders Point and taste the legacy.

Note: Photographs for Traders Point Winery were provided by Kathy Woodhouse.

Wines

Naked Chardonnay

This unoaked dry white has a pleasant, fruit forward taste with a buttery finish. Add to cream soups for a special flavor or pair with panko crusted, broiled salmon.

Normandy Noir

This oaked Bordeaux blend carries hints of dark cherries with a smooth ending. Add to beef stew or pair with a Montreal seasoned grilled steak.

Scat Cat

A sweet Muscato wine, it's perfect to drink alone, or add ginger ale and frozen fruit for a spritzer. It's perfect to serve with a meat, cheese, and sourdough bready tray.

Point Blush

This popular Zinfandel wine is easy on the palate and fruity on the finish. Elegant enough to serve with a Thanksgiving or Christmas dinner, light enough to add to frozen wine slushies.

Recipe

Chardonnay Alfredo Sauce

⅔ cup Traders Point Naked Chardonnay
2 cups heavy whipping cream
1 ½ cup shredded Parmesan cheese
2 cloves garlic, crushed
1 8 oz box of fettucine noodles or
    preferred pasta
Salt and pepper to taste

Directions:

In medium sized saucepan, heat cream on medium low heat, stirring occasionally, for about 15 minutes. Do not boil. Add garlic and stir. Add Parmesan cheese ¼ cup at a time, stirring to melt. Slowly add wine, stirring constantly. Add salt and pepper, stir, and reduce heat while making spaghetti according to package directions. Drain and add to sauce, mix well. Serve with extra Parmesan. You may add, chicken, mushrooms, broccoli, or anything you prefer.

EASLEY WINERY
INDIANAPOLIS

"Great wines are meant to be shared."
– Mark and Meredith Easley

Visiting this fantastic winery in the heart of Indianapolis is experiencing the roots of the resurgence of the wine industry in Indiana. Jack and Joan Easley started planting grapes and making wine in their Indianapolis basement in the late 1960s. Jack, a lawyer, and Joan, a market researcher, began to investigate the possibility of opening a winery. They found out it was illegal at the time. They decided to see if the laws could be changed. Luckily, they found a group of like-minded individuals and they formed the Indiana Wine Growers Guild. In 1971, the law was changed, and Indiana wineries were once again allowed.

Jack and Joan purchased a former ice cream factory in downtown Indianapolis and had their first grape crush in 1974. Still in its original location, Easley winery has now been passed on to the second generation of Easleys; Mark and his wife Meredith. Under their tutelage, the winery is having one of the most successful times in its history. "We traveled the world looking at winery business models," said Meredith Easley. They found problems with the way the winery had been created; they needed more capital. They did parties, dinner, and corporate events, and the winery evolved into more of what they had envisioned. However, the Easleys were there until eleven or twelve at night and they wanted to start a family. They changed the direction of the winery to one of production and customer service. "Quality shot through the roof when we focused on one specific thing," explained Meredith.

Another thing the Easelys did was to cut down on the types of grapes grown. Vineyards are so labor intensive and different varieties take different types of care. The Easleys decided to lease farmland in four different states popular for growing grapes; Indiana, Michigan, New York, and California. "The advantage is we are growing certain types of grapes in the best regions," said Meredith. "It takes high quality grapes to make high quality wine," added Mark. "The managers are fully focused on growing grapes." With someone overseeing the vineyards, the Easleys can aim their gifts for wine and marketing in other directions.

"Each brand is focused to particular palates in certain areas," Explained Meredith. Their Reggae brand is fruity and popular. Their Sweet Tulip brand is light and sweet. The sparkling wines and champagnes are very well received, and the Kauffman brand is regal and traditional. The wine at Easleys is some of the best to be found, but it doesn't compare to their customer service.

"It's not about our ego," said Mark. "It's about making a great experience for our guests. We want everyone who works here to be serious about making the winery successful." Saturdays are so busy that there is always a second tasting bar open. "We want each person to feel as if they're part of a small group tasting experience." This could be seen and heard as guest chanted along with their taste instructor and clapped after various presentations. At Easley, the focus is fully on the customer. The winery draws people in, but the excellent wine and exceptional customer service is what keeps them coming back. We highly suggest you stop by soon for your own small group experience. You'll soon be back.

Note: Photographs for Easley Winery were provided by Kathy Woodhouse.

Easley Winery
205 North College Avenue
Indianapolis, IN 46202
317-636-4516

Events: No

Wine Trail: Indy Wine Trail

Wines

I Think Red Blend

A blend of Merlot and Cabernet Sauvignon is slightly oaked to increase the tannin structure in this gold medal dry wine. Pair with smoked or grilled beef.

Sweet Tulip Moscato

Succulent aromas of orange blossom and lemon zest bloom as you swirl your glass. Serve it chilled with a smoked salmon Caesar salad.

Reggae Blush

Sweet citrus springs forth from Reggae Blush like a geyser of awesomeness. Pair it with light sandwiches and wraps, salmon, or grilled bratwurst.

Warm Mulled Wine

Cozy up by the fire and enjoy a glass of Warm Mulled Wine, rich with cinnamon and apple flavors that, when served warm, spice up your life.

From the Winery

Madeleine's Caprese Salad

2 ripe locally grown Heirloom tomatoes – prefer one red and one yellow

12 oz. Fresh Mozzarella

Large bunch of fresh Basil leaves

2 cups Balsamic Vinegar – reduce to make a glaze or serve as is. I prefer the straight vinegar and not the glaze.

Optional additions:

Sprinkle of olive oil and salt and pepper.

When you have all of your fresh ingredients and are ready to build your Caprese, cut the tomatoes as a cross section into large thick slices,

Arrange them on your favorite platter rotating the colors of the tomatoes. Slice the mozzarella thickly- not thicker than tomato, and make sure you have enough mozzarella to layer onto each tomato slice.

Gently wash basil in a colander or each sprig by hand, lay on a plate that is covered in a paper towel to dry, pat dry. Let air dry for a moment. Pull the leaves off gently and completely and lay on top of the mozzarella.

You should now have a tower of fresh delight! Tomato, Mozzarella, Basil. Each person can have their own serving.

Sprinkle with Balsamic Vinegar or Balsamic Glaze individually or before serving.

Optional:

Drizzle with Olive Oil and a dash of Salt and Pepper

Pair with chilled or room temperature Easley Traminette. This is a great palate lift any time of the year. If you have it in the summer the ingredients are fresh and you feel like you are tasting the best of summer's garden. If you have a Caprese in the winter you feel a freshness and a lift from the heavier foods of winter.

"Our Recipe is your Success"
– Kevin and Tatyana Croak

The motto at Harmony Winery, "Our recipe is your success," may not make sense, until you realize the winery hosts a lot of classes to teach others how to make wine. It's very different and we could find no other wineries offering the same classes. People come and do some wine tasting to decide what they like best. They order juice and once it gets there, people can choose to only start it and let owner Kevin Croak do the rest, or they can be involved in any part of the process. Once the wine is finished, a process that takes anywhere from 4-10 weeks, the customer bottles it, receiving between twenty to thirty bottles, and affixes a custom label. Many people plan this out months in advance for parties, weddings, and/or gift giving. The classes are very popular.

Tatyana Croak is a funny lady and has a big presence at the winery, telling stories and making people laugh. "These are our pet parrots," she said pointing at two toy parrots hanging over the wine bar. "Their names are Jimmy and Buffet. They have little hats they wear at Christmas time."

When asked the reason she likes owning a winery, "My favorite part about owning a winery is that I get to drink wine for free." Tatyana is the reason Kevin restarted his winery path; more about the restarted later. "I bought him a homemaking wine kit as a gift. After he entered two wines in the Indiana State Fair as an amateur winemaker and won medals for both, Kevin was ready to take his wine obsession a bit further. His first experiences with wine would make anyone hesitate about owning a winery, but Kevin and Tatyana jumped in with both feet.

"We lived in New York when I was young," said Kevin. "One summer I broke my wrist so that meant no swimming and not a lot of other summer activities; I was bored. We had some cherry trees and I decided I was going to try and make some cherry wine." He was 13 or 14 at the time and mixed a concoction of cherries, yeast, and sugar, corked it and hid it down inside a stone at the cemetery next to their house. "I didn't know how long to leave it or how combustible wine can be. I went to check on it one day and the cork had popped off with such force it blew that blood red liquid up all over one of the headstones," Kevin laughed. It was a gruesome sight and it took a while for the stains to fade away. He was reminded of his first efforts at wine making any time he walked past the cemetery. That episode doesn't seem to have caused any permanent hesitations because Kevin eagerly tackles many other new experiences at the winery.

In addition to the classes offered for winemaking, Harmony has a lot of things that involve community activities. Every Friday is Open Mic night, and the event has become very popular. They also have Fruit, Wine, Cocktail, and Dessert Parties. Whether your interest lies in drinking, making, or partying with wine, Harmony has something for all.

*Question: How many calories are in
a four ounce glass of wine?*
Answer: Approximately 85.

Easley Winery
7350 Village Square
 Lane Suite 200
Fishers, IN 46038
317-585-9463

Events: Yes, indoor seating
 up to 30

Wine Trail: Cardinal Flight
 Wine Trail

Wines

☙ **"C" Major Cabernet**

A dry, plump, fruity earlier aging grape with bold, deep character and a nicely balanced finish. Pair with meatballs and spaghetti in marinara sauce or a beef brisket.

☙ **Dolce Fiore**

Lush, fruity and delightfully sweet with juicy peach and tropical flavors. Pair with salty foods, vinegar based sauces, or Asian cuisines.

☙ **Pom Pom**

Pomegranate Zinfandel is a slightly spicy, robust blend with a light, fruity finish. It's great with barbecued pork, grilled burgers, or smoked meats and fish.

☙ **Octet**

Wonderful flavors of orange come bursting forth and blend with the dark bittersweet chocolate held up by the ruby port. Pour over cheesecake, chocolate ice cream, or drink alone.

From the Winery

Shrimp Scampi

½ to ¾ cup Harmony Pinot Grigio
1 Pd. box of angel hair pasta
1 Tbl. olive oil
1 Pd. Large shrimp, peeled and deveined, jumbo is best
2-4 cloves of fresh garlic, minced
¼ tsp. salt and fresh ground pepper
5 Tbl. salted butter
¼ cup parsley
1 cup chopped green onion, bulb and stem
Parmesan cheese

Directions:

Add pasta to a large pot of boiling, salted water and cook until ready. While cooking pasta, heat a large skillet over medium-high heat. Add the olive oil and green onion. Cook 1-2 minutes, and then add butter and garlic. When butter is melted, add shrimp and cook 1-2 minutes it becomes pink in color on one side. Flip over, add salt and pepper, wine, and raise the heat to high for 1-2 minutes. Cover with lid 1-2 minutes. Open lid, stir and let sauté 1-2 minutes more. Remove from heat. Drain pasta and place on large serving dish. Pour shrimp and sauce on top and toss to mix together. Top with parsley and Parmesan cheese, or serve cheese on the side.

COUNTRY MOON WINERY
NOBLESVILLE

"Grapevines hold many lessons for life."
– Becky Harger

The first thing visitors will notice while coming up the gravel drive at Country Moon Winery, is the lovely landscape. The plantings resemble an English garden with mature, flowering bushes and smaller, trimmed plants. Although a lot of it was designed, parts of the landscaping aren't so planned out. Co-owner Becky Harger's philosophy about the gardens is to let things grow where they want to go. "If something wants to grow, I let it. A lot of things people consider weeds are actually good butterfly attracters." Becky incorporates this love of nature into the winery itself.

The vineyards and surrounding fields seems to stretch for miles. Though the layout and buildings on the property, including the Harger's log cabin home, might seem simple, they were arranged to enhance the natural world around them.

"People come here from the city and the first thing they do is take a deep breath," said Becky. Brian and Becky Harger planned all construction on the property and the views are intentional. The name of the winery, Country Moon with the crescent moon logo, reflects the importance of their philosophies.

"You can see the horizon in several directions and this affords views of the changing phases of the moon," Becky explained. The moon rises almost an hour later every day. "It beckons us to

110

slow down. We hope when people visit, they can relax and take in the natural, park-like setting." The wine is part of the full experience at Country Moon Winery. The winery is a free-standing arched building with an old-world style brick front. Tastings happen at this charming entrance area or other settings around the property.

"When the weather is nice, we utilize the cabin porch and patio." They also have campfire nights where people come and roast marshmallows. "People bring their chairs and food and just have a great time." We could see why it has become such a favored gathering spot. Bees and butterflies floated over a small garden where an old rusted bicycle leaned against a board fence. It looked as if a child hopped off forty years ago and left it there, but that's by plan. "We rescued it from my uncle's farm when the house and land was sold for development." The Harger's didn't change a thing about the bike, just wanted to keep it as it was to blend in with the rustic atmosphere.

When asked about their foray into the wine business, Becky smiled slightly, as if bringing up a sweet memory. "About fourteen years ago, we started going to wineries. Within a year, we caught the vision of growing our own grapes and opening a winery. Wine is very seductive."

Part of their mission as winery owners is to grow all of their grapes themselves. They currently have five different varieties on two acres. "Grapevines hold many lessons for life. Some of these thoughts are shared in the website's *Vineyard Journal*. I am overwhelmed daily by the beauty of creation and the wisdom of its rhythms."

The Hargers have captured these rhythms in a bottle and offer it to friends, family, and strangers who become friends, who show up on their doorstep.

Country Moon Winery
16222 Prairie Baptist Road
Noblesville, IN 46060
317-773-7942
www.countrymoonwinery.com

Events: Yes, up to 60, outdoor only.

Wines

La Crescent

This golden wine has a smooth apricot flavor with a snappy acidity that's delightful on the tongue. Very versatile and pairs well with Gouda cheese, grilled chicken, and smoked fish; even spicy chili.

Concord

Sweet and easy sipping, this wine is a quintessential American grape, developed in Concord, Massachusetts. It pairs well with salty foods like corned beef or Sausage pizza, but also enhances sweet desserts.

Cynthiana

Also known as Norton, this dry wine has a beautiful ruby red color. It pairs well with smoked and grilled meats, wild game and barbecue and other acidic sauces.

Swenson Red

This wine comes from a grape that is both a table and wine grape. Usually red, it can vary in color depending on the temperature during ripening. This wine pairs with any meal, from pasta with Alfredo sauce to Asian cuisine to Thanksgiving dinner.

From the Winery

Country Moon Sangria

"This sweet and fruity beverage is perfect for a summer evening. The alcohol level will drop by half, so an 8-10 ounce serving is equal to one glass of wine. Our sweetest red wine, Concord Mist, is especially suited for this recipe!"

Makes one gallon of Sangria
64 oz. (2 ½ bottles) Country Moon Concord Mist
32 oz. (1 liter) lemon-lime soda
16 oz. pulpy orange juice
8 oz. (⅔ bottle) grenadine
Ice
Fresh Fruit

Mix all except the ice and fresh fruit. Serve over ice with fresh fruit on a skewer.

MADISON COUNTY WINERY
MARKLEVILLE

In the farming community around Markleville in Central Indiana, sits a cute winery enjoyed by many. Madison County Winery, not to be confused with Madison Vineyards Estate Winery and Bed & Breakfast in the city of Madison, is a welcome respite on a hot day. The gregarious Eric Hensley greeted us like old friends and took us through his wine journey while poking fun at himself the whole time.

"I was an ornery kid," Hensley laughed. "I started making wine, beer, and even moonshine when I was around fourteen. My parents would find it every now and then and pour it out." His parents, Cathy and Duke Hensley, are an integral part of the winery

now, but could never imagine their lives here when they were finding their son's experiments.

"I got better at making it and became legal age," joked Eric. Before becoming a professional wine maker and gaining a license, friends and family started asking if they could buy his wines. Of course, he didn't sell it to them; that's illegal! However, his parents tried it and liked it. This is where the germ of an idea started and Eric considered having a winery someday. "I had a good job," he said. "We always saw it as a future endeavor." However, he lost his job and it seemed like a good time to try the winery idea. His parents, along with his wife, Amber, fully supported him and Madison County Winery opened in 2008.

The winery first started in a storefront in historic Pendleton, nearby. It wasn't long before they were ready to expand, and Duke began construction on the property where the winery now sits. He's a master craftsman who also built the wine bars and the adorable dollhouse in the tasting room, set up for children who may come by. The winery is very family friendly and has a playset outside near the patio so parents can keep a watchful eye. Once the winery was up and running, all family members enthusiastically helped out.

Madison County Winery
10942 South 400 East
Markleville, IN 46056
765-778-1406

Events: Yes, outdoor only,
 up to 100

Trail: Cardinal Flight Wine Trail

Eric's dad Duke jumped in with both feet. "He's the head wine-maker now and loves to experiment with different things." This is why they are, as far as we could find, the only winery in Indiana with a to-mato wine: Duke's Tomato. A white semi-sweet wine, tomatoes have no tannins, thus the white color is only one of the interesting things about this wine. It starts smooth and slightly sweet, then finishes with a light tomato flavor reminiscent of a Bloody Mary. He also makes a pumpkin spice wine and a very popular candy apple cider, both of which were sold out when we visited.

Cathy, Eric's mother, makes the cute and colorful aprons in the gift shop. These can be custom made for special occasions. "I'm the presi-dent on paper," said Eric, "but everyone takes on any role that's neces-sary." That attitude is what makes this family-owned winery work so well. They're all invested to see it succeed. There are even pets that give their all, sort of. "We have angora goats, that's where the yarn comes from we sell." For visitors who want to visit and pet the goats, it's only a short walk.

Madison County Winery is very generous with their patrons. They hold painting parties, giveaways, and allow independent businesses such as Mary Kay and 31 to hold wine and cheese parties for their meetings. Visitors can walk the vineyard, enjoy the scenery from the porch or share in stories and conversation with the Hensleys. What-ever your favorite wine-centered activity, Madison County Winery can fill every need.

Wines

❧ Puerto Concordia

This port-style wine is 18% alcohol, so serve in small glasses as an aperitif or pour over your favorite cake for a yummy new treat.

❧ Duke's Tomato

This port-style wine is 18% alcohol, so serve in small glasses as an aperitif or pour over your favorite cake to for a yummy new treat.

❧ Chardonnay

A luscious, buttery dry white. This is the wine to pull out for special guests or a romantic dinner for two of Coq au vin.

❧ Candy Apple

A sweet wine unique to Madison County Winery. Serve with salads containing fresh berries and almonds.

Pairing

Madison County Winery's Love Potion #9 pairs well with the Milani Pot Roast on page 81. (T.J. Haase's recipe.) We recommend this delicious dry concord with any beef dish.

BELGIAN HORSE WINERY
MIDDLETOWN

Although this is one of Indiana's newest wineries, opening in January of 2016, there is a long history of work and wine at Belgian Horse Winery and owner Jerri Harter has worked hard to keep the feel of the past alive. When visitors pull into the winery, they are greeted by the sight of a creatively refurbished barn that the owners of Belgian Horse Winery cleverly turned into a tasting room and event space. The arched doorway extends up through the roof of the porch for an aesthetic view that combines old world architecture with modern charm, while the stone façade hints at years of agricultural strength.

The timbers were from the original structure and they were pressure washed and left in place. The seating area was once a milking parlor and the upstairs event area with a lovely barrel shaped ceiling, used to be the hay loft.

It's a little murky how the first ancestor, William Fleming, came to the decision to buy this piece of land in the middle of Indiana. He was a soldier in the Revolutionary War and had settled in Virginia before moving to Indiana. His son, William Fleming II bought the land from him and was quite famous in relation to his Civil War service and battles with General Sherman. He's written about in Hazzard's History of Henry County published in 1905. Harry Harter, grandfather of current owner, Jerri Harter, raised and sold Belgian horses, as well as using them on the farm.

Belgian horses are a draft horse breed that can grow up to 2,000 pounds. They are used for pulling heavy loads and are especially prized for pulling wagons and plows, making them the perfect companion to farming.

In 1943, Harry Harter brought recognition to the area when his horses, Roc and Doc, won the World Draft Horse-Pulling Championship. Breeders and farmers, including many Amish, wanted

Belgian Horse Winery
7200 West CR 625 Nor
Middletown, IN 47356
765-779-3002

Events: Yes, indoors up
Outdoors, unlimited.

their famous bloodline and came to Middletown, Indiana in droves to purchase the colts from Roc and Doc's lineage. The impact the family tradition has had on the winery can be seen in the names and photos on the labels, in the winery, and with the name itself. It's a way to honor the past while looking toward the future.

There is a long history of sharing time and wine with family within the Harter clan and the winery became an extension of this. There's a pineapple wine named Charlie, a Midnight Molly Blend, a Spring-time Puppy Blend, and many horse themed labels. Animals are family too at Belgian Horse Winery. The people at the winery enjoy sharing their space and stories with any and all visitors, but the building is truly a work of art.

Three generations of family built the heavy wooden staircase from a tree on the property. They milled the wood and even built a kiln to fire it. The family's pride in their agricultural heritage can not only be seen in the care taken to re-create the barn, but in the fact that 99% of the work in the building was accomplished by family members.

They invite all visitors to come and share in their history and stories, but don't get so caught up in them that you forget to sample the wine. It's fantastic.

Wines

Cabernet Franc

This dry, savory wine has medium-high acidity and a wonderful mouth feel. Pair with savory, bold flavors such as a marinara sauce with green peppers or chili seasoned with cinnamon, cumin, and cloves.

Pineapple Wine

Sweet and refreshing. This unusual wine dances on the tongue and has a slight floral on the nose. Create a unique wine punch using ½ glass of wine, ½ glass of peach nector, and add mandarin orange slices.

Catawba

A semi-sweet wine with just the right hint of sweet and tart, pair this versatile wine with everything from pizza and burgers to an elegant prime rib roast.

Muscat

Light and sweet, this wine is the one to serve at a backyard appetizer party or girls' dinner.

Recipe

Happy Fruit

You can use almost any preferred wine with this recipe, but we prefer the semi-sweet to sweet or port-style and ice wines.

1 cup of Belgian Horse Pineapple Wine
3 cups of preferred fruit mix

Stir the wine into the fruit. You can serve immediately or let the fruit soak to absorb more of the wine. Serve over a green salad, on the side of a slice of cake or pie, or as a fruit salad. The fruit can also be frozen to add to a glass of wine to keep it cool and not dilute the flavor.

TONNE WINERY
MUNCIE

"We want people to enjoy."
– Kevin & Mary Tonne, Larry and Kathie Simmons

Tonne (rhymes with Sunny) Winery is the brain-child of brothers-in-law Kevin Tonne and Larry Simmons, who put their interests in horticulture and food science together and started an adventure known as owning a winery.

"We started this as a business venture," explained Kevin Tonne, who had no previous wine making experiences. "We fell in love with making wine and meeting so many people; we wish we'd opened five years earlier."

What first drew Larry Simmons's attention to the burgeoning wine industry in Indiana was his cousin David Simmons's winery in Columbus, Indiana. He noticed there were no wineries in the Muncie area, and he liked the way his cousin had utilized the family farm, keeping it agriculture and sustaining it there on the homestead. He approached his brother-in-law, Kevin Tonne, who has a food science degree. He was on board pretty quickly and 53 weeks after the idea was agreed upon, Tonne Winery officially opened.

"We did our homework," said Kevin. During the time of building, they visited wineries and attended seminars to learn all they could about the business. "Seven years ago when we first decided we were going to do this," Kevin imparted, "there were forty-three wineries; now there are over eighty."

The Indiana winery industry's recent explosion can be attributed to several factors, all of them good. The team at Purdue is always available to wineries to help them with advice and marketing, but it's the other wineries' attitudes that really helped. "The wineries were so generous in sharing their knowledge with us," complimented Kevin. "All the wineries help each other." We've seen this before in communities where everyone helps everyone else, all benefit. Another way Tonne Winery helps the community is by continuously carrying a large display from various local artists in their 1,500 square foot tasting room. This and the cute and modern tables and chairs makes visitors feel as if they've entered a French bistro to sample wines and enjoy conversation with friends; which is what the people at Tonne become to guests.

"It gives us so much satisfaction when people come back to visit us because of the wines we've developed and the customer service they've experienced," said Tonne. We know we've made some lifelong friends who we will be visiting again and again. We hope to see you there.

"I will drink no wine before it's time. It's time!"
– Groucho Marx

Tonne Winery
101 Royerton Road
Muncie, IN 47303
765-896-9821

Events: Yes, indoors only;
  up to 50

Trail: The Wineries of Indiana's
  Northeast Tour

Wines

❧ Kabrie

A blend of four Bordeaux wines resulting in a nice, dry, lightly oaked fruit forward flavor. Serve with red meats or pasta. If you have a sense of humor, you might ask what we think "Kabrie" stands for.

❧ Pinot Grigio

This white wine is filled with classic Italian flavors and well-balanced between dry and crisp. It compliments most light Italian and vegetable dishes.

❧ Royerton Red

This delightful red wine bursts with the traditional fruity grape flavors. Sweet enough to serve anytime; serve it chilled with desserts, especially chocolate.

❧ Cranberry

A nice balance of traditional cranberry aroma, flavor, and sweetness, this wine is a pleasant accompaniment to Thanksgiving dinner, or any chicken or pork dish.

Recipe

Best Lasagna Ever

2 cups Tonne Winery Chambourcin wine, plus more for pairing

4 - 15 oz. cans Italian tomatoes

1 pound sweet Italian ground sausage (this can be made meatless, if preferred)

2 cloves of garlic, crushed

1 14 oz. container of ricotta cheese

1 8 oz. container cream cheese with chives

3 cups shredded mozzarella cheese, divided

½ cup shredded Parmesan cheese

2 eggs

1 16 oz. package of lasagna noodles, cooked according to package directions

Directions:

In medium bowl, combine ricotta cheese, cream cheese and chive, 1 cup of mozzarella cheese, and two eggs, mix well. Refrigerate for at least three hours. While cheese mixture is in refrigerator, combine wine, tomatoes, and garlic in deep skillet over medium-high heat. Cook, smashing tomatoes to create a chunky sauce, about 15-20 minutes. Turn on low and allow to simmer until cheeses are ready. When time has elapsed, turn oven to 375° and brown Italian sausage. Drain well, and add to sauce. Cook noodles according to package directions. Assemble by spreading four tablespoons of sauce in the bottom of 9x13 pan. Place three or four noodles on top, spread ½ cheese mixture over noodles. Place more noodles on top, spread with ½ remaining sauce, sprinkle with 1 cup mozzarella and ¼ cup of parmesan. Layer once more in the same order, finishing with the rest of the sauce, mozzarella, and parmesan cheeses. Cover with aluminum foil, making sure not to touch cheese. Bake 45 minutes, removing aluminum foil for the last 15. Serve with salad, garlic bread, and Tonne Winery Chambourcin wine.

J&J WINERY & NOBLE ORDER BREWING COMPANY
RICHMOND

"Join the craft crusade"
– Melody and Jeff Haist

Sitting on a beautiful spot of land in Central Indiana is a must visit spot; J&J Winery and Noble Order Brewing Company. We would suggest a visit just for the different types of wine and beer alone, but there's so much more to this winery that visitors must see. A fountain cascades into a lake, creating rainbows as it showers down. Arches covered with vines and different leveled decks and patios afford views of the landscaped gardens and lovely hillsides. The unspoiled natural surroundings aren't the only attractions at J&J.

A large wood-fired oven dominates an area of the upper patio. This brick structure was ordered from

Italy and brought by truck from California to Richmond, Indiana. "That's one thing my husband really wanted to do," explained part-owner Melody Haist. "He wanted everything to be authentic. Everything is fresh made. We smoke pork for bacon and pork sandwiches. We grow our own vegetables and we make our own dough daily." Despite the fact that the winery looks as if it was always planned for this spot, as it blends perfectly with the surroundings, the idea of having a winery is a newer concept for Melody and Jeff.

"We bought the 1920s' farmhouse in 2008 and just kept adding on over the years," said Melody. In 2004, while Jeff Haist and his neighbor Jim were sharing a bottle of wine, it was suggested that they should plant grapes and try making wine. Though neither had ever grown grapes or made wine, it seemed like a good idea. They planted some grapes and tried their hand at making wine. Jim and Jeff were both avid gardeners, but grapes are a different type of animal, and they struggled at first. While waiting for the grapes to produce a healthy crop, which can take years of careful pruning and care, they learned how to make wine. They started in the basement but along the way to the first successful crop of 2008, they'd decided to open a business and J&J Winery, named for the first initials

J&J Winery
3415 National Road West
Richmond, IN 47374
765-965-9463 (Wine)

Events: Yes, small gatherings;
no weddings.

of Jim and Jeff, opened in 2009. "In 2010, I retired from my regular job to run the winery full time," Melody said. The Noble Order Brewing Company and Gemstone Café followed soon after. They threw themselves into making the business a success and it shows in their customer service and attention to detail.

The winery carries fifteen varietals, with five of them estate grown. "Apple Ambrosia is my go to bonfire wine," said employee Stephanie Fox. The brewery carries fourteen, European influenced beers, including Blood Orange, Belgium Double, Scotch Ale, and Bad to the Boone, to represent Boone County. In addition to the liquid refreshments, the Gemstone Café offers something for everyone.

From appetizers, which includes their wood fired bread sticks, to hearty pastas and pizzas, even the pickiest member of the family will find something he or she likes. Finish that off with cheesecake and wine on the deck overlooking the lake and you'll think you've found Eden; you just may have.

Wines

Vesuvius Shiraz

This full-bodied and fruity dry red wine has soft tannins and a bouquet of blackberries highlighted with light pepper and plum flavors. This wine will enhance a meal of deer, garlic mashed potatoes, and roasted carrots, parsnips, and cauliflower.

Apple Ambrosia

This local apple cider infused with spices and cinnamon is a silver medal winner. Serve hot or cold or add it to meat dishes to make a marinade or sauce.

Athena Muscat

The sweet white wine is medium-bodied with lingering floral flavors. It pairs well with ice creams, puddings, pastries, fresh fruits, and full-flavored cheeses.

Dionysus Delight

This dark, sweet wine is the perfect blend of dark chocolate and raspberry. Fruit cobblers and flavored cakes compliment this wine very well.

Recipe

Ambrosia Hummus Salad

¼ cup J & J Apple Ambrosia Wine
1 cup plain hummus
½ Tbl. Smoked paprika
½ Tbl. Sesame seeds
1 Tbl. Parsley
1 pound chicken strips
3 Tbl. Olive oil
1 red bell pepper, chopped
1 small sweet onion, sliced thin
1 15 oz. can artichokes, drained
1 pound various fresh greens, spinach, lettuces, etc.

Directions:

Wash fresh greens and place in large bowl. In medium skillet, cook chicken, onion, and red pepper until chicken is cooked through. Add hummus, wine, artichokes, sesame seeds, paprika, and spices. Stir to heat. Pour over greens and serve immediately.

BUCK CREEK WINERY
INDIANAPOLIS

"Make good wine and be friendly."
– Jeff and Amy Durm

Jeff and Amy Durm's wine journey began more than twenty-five years ago. "I started visiting wineries in Ohio," Jeff explained, "and fell in love with this one owned by a doctor. I thought, 'Wow, if they can make good wines in the middle of Ohio, why can't I make good wines in the middle of Indiana?'" In 1991, Jeff first planted some grape vines. "Relatives on my mother's side are farmers, and I've always had my hands in the soil," he stated. He also started playing around with wine making. Although certain for many years he would start a winery, he held off taking the plunge.

"I wanted to get a pension from the police department before depending on the winery as an income," Durm said. It wasn't long before Durm planted more vines and started selling grapes to wineries. "The agricultural lifestyle is something that always appealed to me." Along with deciding which grapes would grow best on his Indianapolis land, Durm became more serious with his winemaking, trying different types of fruits other people don't necessarily think of when making wine, such as rhubarb. He didn't keep all of the wine for his own needs. "I made wine and we donated some to our church. We still do today." Some of his early winemaking turned out well, others not so much.

While continuing his experimentations, Jeff felt he needed to gain more experience. "I went to Dr. Thomas from Chateau Thomas winery. I introduced myself and said, 'I'd like to work for you because eventually I'd like to own my own winery.' They just stared at me unimpressed. Then I said, 'I'll work for free.' They said, 'You're hired.'" Durm

laughed. Jeff learned the craft through a mixture of Dr. Thomas, Thomas's son Steven, who owns Thomas Family Winery in Madison, and his own ideas.

He planted the only vineyard in the city of Indianapolis, and Buck Creek Winery opened in 2006 so the Durms could share the results of Jeff's efforts with the world. "I started out with four wines, but knew I had to have the full range from dry to sweet in order to satisfy everyone's tastes." Another must was the label. All of the wine labels have a buck deer on them, all that is except for one named after the Durm's daughter, Rocio. Their sons work at the winery and there are wines containing their names too.

Since opening with their original four offerings, the Durms have expanded their selections to more than twenty-five wines. "If you find people's taste preference," exclaimed Jeff, "we'll have a wine they like." We saw this for ourselves shortly after we arrived when the room filled with patrons, all eager to share in the wine experiences available at Buck Creek Winery.

A bridal party came in with many happy and laughing ladies ready for a day of fun and pampering. There was a couple on a wine trail, and several regulars came in to get their favorite bottle. They may have all come in separately, but it looked like one big party for other visitors coming into the tasting room. Whatever the reason, Jeff and Amy Durm invite you to come and share in their lovely winery.

Buck Creek Winery
11747 Indian Creek Road South
Indianapolis, IN 46259
317-862-9463

Events: Yes, indoors up to 60; outdoors up to 100

Trail: Indy Wine Trail

Wines

⚜ Zinfandel

This full-bodied and fruity dry red wine has soft tannins and a bouquet of blackberries highlighted with light pepper and plum flavors. A meal with deer, garlic mashed potatoes, and roasted carrots, parsnips, and cauliflower, will enhance this wine.

⚜ Forget Me Not

A white wine made from the Traminette grape; it has a lovely floral aroma with honey, apple, and grapefruit flavors. Add to cream based soups or pair with seafood.

⚜ Rocio

This bubbly Catawba wine has luscious, fruity flavors and pairs well with cheese and fruit. Great for an appetizer party, light fish, or even cheese and crackers.

⚜ Alley Cat

Alley Cat has flavors and aromas of cranberries and strawberries, with a slightly spicy finish. Great to add to chili to eat or for chili dogs, or Thanksgiving dinner.

Recipe

Chili Dog Sauce

Adding wine to your chili or chili dog sauce really kicks the flavors up a notch.

¾ cup Buck Creek's Alley Cat Wine
2 pounds lean ground beef
2 cups ketchup
¼ cup mustard
½ sweet onion, chopped
1 tsp. Worcestershire sauce
½ tsp fresh ground pepper
½ tsp kosher salt
2 Tbl. Butter

In large, deep skillet, melt butter and sauté onions until they begin to brown. Add ground beef, brown and drain. Mix in salt and pepper thoroughly. Add all other ingredients and let cook until thickened. Serve over hotdogs with whatever toppings you prefer. Mine is sharp cheddar cheese and mustard. Yummy!

MALLOW RUN WINERY
BARGERSVILLE

"Work hard; picnic often"

In 1835, George Mallow settled the farm that eventually became Mallow Run Winery. Mallow's great-great grandson, co-owner, John Richardson grew up on the farm, went away to college, and then taught English in New Albany for thirty-five years. He retired to the farm with the intention of growing grapes for other Indiana wineries. The first vines were planted in 2000. John had been an amateur wine maker, so he, and his son Bill, used some of the grapes for some of their early creations. Another reason John Richardson chose to move back to the 600 acre farm is that he hoped to keep more generations of the family interested in an agricultural lifestyle. He needn't have worried about that.

Bill grew up dreaming of living on the farm. He settled into the original homestead after graduating from Purdue with a degree in agriculture. More than 50,000 bushels of corn and soybeans are still raised each year on the farm, in addition to the grapes. While playing in the Carmel symphony, Bill met Laura Emerson, who was also interested in wine. It wasn't long before the two were married. With the vineyards taking root, the

Richardsons explored the feasibility of opening a winery in Central Indiana.

They wanted to keep the home-farm winery feel as much as possible and converted the 1870s' era barn on the property into a beautiful tasting room. "We had to lower the basement floor 14 inches in order to fit the tanks," explained John. When they started, the business plan was to open a separate production room in four to five years; they built it in eighteen months. On September 3rd, 2005, Mallow Run Winery opened to the public. This was Labor Day weekend and the Richardsons celebrate each year now by hosting a very popular three day pig roast with bands and lots of food.

From the beginning, Mallow Run had more guests than expected. "We hoped to grow," said John. "We just didn't expect to grow this fast." He isn't complaining though and loves to "schmooze with customers," as he puts it. "We've had people from all over the country. One lady from Mississippi swore a wine she tasted was from a Muscadine grape," a local grape in Mississippi, "when it actually was a Niagara." Adding to their notoriety, Mallow Run Winery was featured in a Wall Street Journal article about how wineries sustain themselves during the winter months when business is slow. "We have winter warm-up weekends with homemade soups and breads January through March," John said. Despite the weather being so cold, people want to get out and these weekends have proved to be very popular. This commitment to the customer has led the Richardsons into new territories.

They decide on their offerings based on their customers' likes and requests. "Customers were asking for beer." With micro-breweries very popular now, many wineries are adding beers to their list of products. Mallow Run developed a hard cider, which is now being served, and they have a hopped cider, as well. This willingness to listen to their customer base and always looking toward developing new additions for the winery, has led them to a devoted following.

Because of this, they're always finding new ways to share the winery with the public. There's Sip & Stitch a few nights a month, where people come to knit and sip wine. Cork & Canvas is a popular painting event, and the popular Picnic Concert Series offers food, wine, and music on weekends from late May through September.

With their many award winning wines, ciders, great foods, and great customer service, you'll find yourself returning time and again to this gem of a winery.

Mallow Run Winery
6964 West Whiteland Road
Bargersville, IN 46106
317-422-1556

Events: Yes, up to 400 at their beautiful separate facility, The Sycamore, plus other events at the winery nearly every weekend throughout the year.

Wines

Vino Rosso

A blend of Cabernet Sauvignon, Sangiovese, and Chambourcin grapes, this wine is reminiscent of the Tuscan-style wines of Italy. Notes of balanced blueberry and strawberry are highlighted by a subtle oak influence.

Picnic White

This sweet wine is a blend of Cayuga and Diamond grapes. Fresh tropical aromas with hints of pear and mango make this a customer favorite.

Cayuga

Riesling like aromas and flavors of Granny Smith apples are highlighted in this light-bodied white wine. Pairs with most cheeses, cured meats, and sweets.

Rhubarb

Sweet but with that unique rhubarb zing on the end. Try it with a cheese plate, green salad or pasta salad.

Recipe

Peachy-Keen Rhubarb Cobbler

½ cup Mallow Run Rhubarb Wine
6 cups peeled and sliced fresh peaches (frozen will work too)
1 cup brown sugar
1 tsp. cinnamon
½ stick butter
1 ready-made pie crust
Cinnamon and sugar for sprinkling

Directions:

Melt butter in large, deep skillet. Add wine, peaches, brown sugar, and 1 tsp. cinnamon. Cook until peaches are softened and sauce starts to thicken. Pour into 13 x 9 cake pan. Top with crust, sprinkle with cinnamon and sugar. Bake in a 350° oven for 25-30 minutes.

CHATEAU THOMAS WINERY
PLAINFIELD

"for the discriminating wine enthusiast"
– Dr. Charles Thomas

The impressive winery and tasting room at Chateau Thomas peeks out from behind shops and greenery as you're driving down I-70, west of Indianapolis. The French chateau style building perfectly encompasses all of the wonderful things that make this winery definitely worth the visit.

Upon entering, a white statue of Pomona, the Roman goddess of fruitful abundance, stands in the tiled foyer. The legend is that she watches over and protects fruits to ensure a bountiful harvest. Large barrel shaped trophy cases adorn both sides of the double doored entrance and hold some of the many awards Chateau Thomas Winery has won at both national and international competitions. These include the Tasters Guild International in Grand Rapids, Michigan and the International Eastern Wine Competition in the storied Finger Lakes region of New York state. All of this notoriety began with a simple hobby by Dr. Charles Thomas.

In the 1970s, Thomas was intrigued by the very beginnings of the resurgence of the wine industry in Indiana. He decided then that he wanted to be a part of it, but he was meticulous about research. "I took some formal winemaking and wine-tasting courses." Wine tasting courses may seem obscure, but wine is both simple and complex. Simple in that it takes so few ingredients to

Chateau Thomas Winery
6291 Cambridge Way
Plainfield, IN 46168
317-837-9463

Tasting Room:
225 South Van Buren Street
Nashville, IN 47448
812-988-8500 or 888-761-9463

Events: Yes, up to 350

Trail: Indy Wine Trail

make it, juice, sugar, and yeast, but complex in that it takes a myriad of conditions to create truly spectacular wine.

Along with the courses, Thomas studied the finest French wines to understand what made them different from other wines. Judges look for specific things when rating wines. Balance is one component. They are checking to see that no one feature, sweetness, tannins, acidity, and alcohol, does not overpower another. Length-the taste lasts all the way on the palate- is another feature plus depth, a mouth feel that can be described as light, medium, or full-bodied, and complexity, a wine that is surprising in its flavors and how it lingers on the tongue and how it finishes, round out the judging standards. After this, Thomas traveled to Napa to learn under some of the most renowned winemakers there. Although he began studying the wine industry in the 1970s, he and his wife Jill did not launch Chateau Thomas Winery until 1984.

Opening on the South side of Indianapolis, Chateau Thomas quickly leapt into a must-see winery on many lists. Dr. Thomas's commitment to the craft resulted in the growth of the winery so that it doubled in size and now includes a 4,000 square foot banquet room, a large gift shop, and an outdoor venue for entertainment. From humble beginnings, Chateau Thomas Winery now makes 50 different varieties of wine and bottles over 15,000 cases each year. Although this is an astounding number, "the mission of the winery is to always pursue quality instead of volume."

One of his selections has become very popular for a variety of reasons. Their Slender® brand wine is a newer idea in the industry and seems to fill a niche that was missing. It's the world's first naturally-sweetened carb-free wine. It gained national attention and was even included in the gift bags given out at the 81st annual Academy Awards.

Although Chateau Thomas Winery has garnered so much recognition that Thomas could relax and let others run the winery, he's there nearly every day talking to people, conducting wine tours, and just sharing his love of wine with others. Drop by and learn from him sometime soon.

Wines

Pinot Noir

Aromas of dark cherries, strawberry, raspberry, are framed by chocolate in this unique wine. Pair with beef stew or roast duck, and casseroles.

Verdelho

A crisp, dry, mineral-laden white wine originating in Portugal. Aromas of peach, lime, honeysuckle and limestone are seen in this full-bodied wine; perfect for salads, seafood, and fowl.

Slender Blush

Strawberry aromas with a beautiful pink color, this wine is pleasantly sweet and pairs well with chocolate and light shrimp dishes.

Late-Harvest Viognier

Floral aromas with apple, citrus, and strong, boisterous character are the highlights of this dessert wine. Serve as a dessert or with tart, berry desserts.

From the Winery

Ginger Scallops

½ cup Chateau Thomas Winery Chardonnay
1 ¼ pounds medium-size scallops, seared in butter
2 Tbls finely chopped green onion
2 Tbls butter
2 Tbls finely chopped fresh ginger
1 large carrot, julienned
½ cup whipping cream
Freshly ground salt and pepper, to taste

Directions:

In a medium skillet over med-high heat, melt one tablespoon of butter and sauté green onion. Add the carrots and cook for thirty seconds, add ginger, then stir in the wine. When thoroughly heated, add the cream, salt, pepper, and cook over high heat until the sauce is reduced by half. Add scallops and cook one minute. Turn off heat, add one tablespoon of butter and serve. If preferred, you may serve over your favorite rice or pasta.

The South Central Region

WINDY KNOLL WINERY • *Vincennes, Knox County*

CAROUSEL WINERY • *Mitchell, Lawrence County*

OLIVER WINERY • *Downtown 812-822-0466*

OWEN VALLEY WINERY • *Spencer, Owen County*

BUTLER WINERY AND VINEYARDS • *Bloomington, Monroe County*

OLIVER WINERY & VINEYARDS • *Bloomington, Monroe County*

CEDAR CREEK WINERY & BREW CO. • *Martinsville, Morgan County*

BROWN COUNTY WINERY DOWNTOWN • *Nashville, Brown County*

SIMMONS WINERY & 450 NORTH BREWING CO. • *Columbus, Bartholomew County*

SALT CREEK WINERY • *Freetown, Jackson County*

CHATEAU DE PIQUE • *Seymour, Jackson County*

STREAM CLIFF HERB FARM TEAROOM & WINERY • *Commiskey, Jennings County*

MADISON VINEYARDS ESTATE WINERY AND BED & BREAKFAST • *Madison, Jefferson County*

LANTHIER WINERY • *Madison, Jefferson County*

THOMAS FAMILY WINERY • *Madison, Jefferson County*

THE RIDGE WINERY • *Vevay, Switzerland County*

FIEKERT'S HOMESTEAD WINES • *Rising Sun, Ohio County*

POWERS' WINERY • *Dillsboro, Dearborn County*

HOLTKAMP WINERY • *New Alsace, Dearborn County*

AT THE BARN WINERY • *Lawrenceburg, Dearborn County*

CHATEAU POMIJE • *Guilford, Dearborn County*

ERTEL CELLARS WINERY • *Batesville, Ripley County*

Additional Wineries
(see page 294 for information)

BROWN COUNTY WINERY • *812-988-6144*
BUTLER WINERY "IN TOWN" TASTING ROOM • *812-339-7233*
CEDAR CREEK TASTING ROOM • *812-988-1111*
CHATEAU THOMAS WINERY NASHVILLE TASTING ROOM • *812-988-8500*
OWEN VALLEY WINERY AT THE TIVOLI MOVIE THEATER • *812-828-0883*
THE RIDGE WINERY TASTING ROOM • *812-427-3380*

WINDY KNOLL WINERY
VINCENNES

The adorable tasting room at Windy Knoll Winery is a place to relax and enjoy. We spied an old time bicycle wine rack we wanted to take with us, but it wouldn't fit in the car. The wine bottle creations come from owner Gwen Leser. "I like to be creative. I melt the bottles down and use them to hold crackers, candy, and cheese, and as spoon rests, whatever people would like to use them for." She is the one in charge of finding unique gift items for the winery, too, such as the bicycle and Eiffel Tower wine holders. She's also the visionary behind the clever gift basket designs. One recent basket, for Nurses' Day, was set up in a doctor's bag.

Years ago, Leser would have laughed if anyone suggested she would be a winery owner one day. She was happy with her ceramic studio and other artistic pursuits. That began to change when she found the perfect Christmas gift for her husband Rick; a wine making kit. "He'd always been an avid wine drinker and traveled throughout Europe sampling the offerings of different wine regions." He happily began his experimentations, and when they built their home in 1994, they also planted their first vines. He was very interested in the noble vinifera vines. There are six types of grapes that are considered the noble vinifera: Chardonnay, Riesling, Pinot Noir, Sauvignon Blanc, and Cabernet. The reasons they are considered noble vinifera are varied. For some of them, the grapes grow easily in a variety of climates and soils, so they're easier to grow and proliferate throughout the world. Pinot Noir is not one of these and is often called the heartbreak grape, because it is one of the hardest to grow. Many of these received their noble title, because they're prolific in wine regions of France and are part

144

of a lot of peoples' first wine experiences. Because of Rick's experiences in Europe, this is where he wanted to start.

Rick was enthusiastic about winemaking from the start and made a lot of wine. Because of this, within four years those first few vines had grown to over seven hundred. It was then the discussion started about opening a winery. "It seemed like a logical next step after acquiring so much wine equipment," said Gwen. In 2001, after the decision was made, they purchased 37 acres, with fourteen currently planted in vines, and Gwen's ceramic shop became the winery. Windy Knoll Winery opened its doors on June 15, 2002. The name of the winery came about because the vineyard is planted on a high knoll and there is always a breeze blowing.

Sadly, Rick is gone now and Toby Williamson has become the vintner and vineyard worker. "We're always working on something, pruning, bottling… we lost some vines this winter and the past four winters have been hard on the vines." When this happens, vines have to be removed and replaced, adding another layer to the work that must be done to keep a commercial winery operating. "Weed control is a big concern," explained Toby. "Too much spraying affects the grapes and can kill vines, as they're sensitive to weed killer. Farmers will sometimes plant grape vines as a gauge for other crops to avoid over spraying them." With great care comes great wines though, and the people at Windy Knoll are set on this goal.

They offer ten varieties of wine made from their own grapes, and six others made using grapes from local growers. Even with all of the care taken to create a variety of wines and their excellent customer service, Gwen worried few people would visit the winery. "Build it and they will come," she laughed quoting the movie "Field of Dreams". "A lot of locals and tourists come to see us regularly." We suggest you go to see them too.

Windy Knoll Winery
845 Atkinson Road
Vincennes, IN 47591
812-726-1600

Events: Yes, indoor only,
  up to 30

Wines

DeChaunac

Rich and deep-bodied, herbal, hints of tobacco and plum, this dry red is available in limited quantities. Serve it with an elegant crown roast or rack of lamb.

Seyval

This grape has the heritage of the Chardonnay family. A white wine with a soft, buttery-oak body and finishes with a hint of green apple. Serve with creamy soups.

Blush

A sweet, delicate wine with flavors of grape. It's light and refreshing and pairs with almost any salad, cheese, or bread.

Summer Strawberry

This wine tastes as if it's fresh from the patch. Loaded with strawberry flavor, add it to strawberries for a strawberry shortcake.

Recipe

The winery gave us a tip and we ran with it. They suggested adding their Summer Strawberry wine instead of the water or milk in boxed brownies or cake mixes. We like to make the cake mix taste more like homemade by adding one extra egg than it calls for and an egg yolk. (Refrigerate the white and add it to scrambled eggs.) Also, switch the oil for melted butter and double it. For example, if the boxed mix asks for ¼ cup of oil, add ½ cup of melted butter. Add any icing you prefer. Yum!

CAROUSEL WINERY
MITCHELL

We at Carousel Winery believe that wine, like life, should be an adventure. Full of the rich varieties that our bountiful earth has to offer, our wine is a tribute to the pristine beauty of nature. We invite you to pause for a moment...step onto the carousel and allow yourself to be swept away in the thrill of living, and the tastes of life.
– Marion and Sue Wilson

Vineyards hung full as we drove up the gravel drive to this winery out in the beautiful countryside of Mitchell, Indiana. Red, a ginger cat, often comes out to greet visitors, but is just as likely to lay in the sunshine and watch as someone walks by. Carousel sits in a picturesque setting with rolling hills, picnic tables, and a pond. The small, family-owned winery has been open since 2003. The owners, Marion & Sue Wilson, handcraft the wine. When it comes to finishing, bottling, and labeling, the whole family gets involved. They also help out whenever they go to events away from the winery such as fairs. Son Shawn and daughter Dawn are the executive vice presidents of marketing, and Marion is the micro-wholesale distributor. Shawn's wife Vicki is the sales executive and is an integral part of the winery. Close friend of the family, Ronnie Hock, a world renowned singer and songwriter who has entertained at the winery, is Carousel's goodwill ambassador. Their

granddaughter, Whitney, lives outside the area, but checks in to see how things are going, and grandson Tyler assists at festivals, making Carousel Winery a whole family affair.

Carousel Winery has been voted one of the top ten wineries in the state of Indiana by Heartland Magazine readers. When standing at the carved limestone tasting bar, visitors will often find unique varieties that mirror the local produce. Red Tiger Red is their most popular wine made from the sweet Concord grape. It's the perfect game day wine and pairs with pizza, burgers, or is just a great sipping wine. White Dove White is a lovely addition to any wedding. Watermelon is very popular and Blueberry and Shadow Dog Port can be found leaving the winery by the case.

The Wilsons also like to experiment with other types of wine. "We make a lot of wines that aren't often seen in this part of Indiana," said Sue, part owner along with husband Marion. "We have a Sangiovese and an Aglianico." Both of these are dry reds that originated in Italy. Medals hung all over the tasting room telling the story of many competitions and contests. But it wasn't always so easy for the Wilsons to make award winning wine.

"We had very little experience with wine making when we first started," explained Sue. However, they come from a generation that is not afraid of anything. Marion is a World War II veteran whose ship, the USS Neches, was sunk off the coast of Hawaii on January 23, 1942, and they took on this new venture with gusto. They did a lot of studying and research about the differences in dry, semi-sweet and sweet wines and the best way to create them to please a variety of palates. "We also took classes and were eager to learn them quickly."

The Wilsons were fast learners, as evidenced by how quickly their wines became popular with the public and all of the international medals they have won. A chef from Indianapolis was so impressed with the wine that he bought a case to hand out to friends.

Another part of Carousel Winery is their involvement in community events. On the weekend before Thanksgiving, they're regular vendors at the Ferdinand ChristKindlmarkt. This Christmas market is a German tradition that attracts thousands of visitors each year to an array of events and goodies including handmade treasures in the Bavarian shopping stalls, an antiques market, and free concerts. Whether it's a fall road trip, a summer concert, or a spring outing, whatever the season, Carousel Winery is definitely worth the visit.

Carousel Winery
6058 Lawrenceport Road
Mitchell, IN 47446
812-849-1005
877-A-WINE-4-U

Events: No

Wines

❧ Cabernet Franc
One of the lightest of the dry reds, toasty aromas and lighter tannins are best paired with lighter meals and good friends.

❧ Lady Luck
This blush wine is just the right mixture of semi-sweet delight. Pair it with chicken salad, light soups, and crusty bread.

❧ White Dove White
A floral aroma and smooth texture highlight the fruitful finish of this white blend. Great for a white sangria mixed with peach juice.

❧ Watermelon
Like biting into the ripest summer fruit, this easy sipping wine is a best seller.

From the Winery

Cherry-Go-Rounds Gelatin Cups

2 cups Carousel Winery Cherry Wine
2 cups Carousel Winery Blueberry Wine
1 small box cherry gelatin
1 small box blueberry gelatin
1 container of whipped topping
Cherries and blueberries for garnish

Make gelatin according to package directions, replacing water with wine. Pour into small plastic cups and place in refrigerator to set. Once set, decorate with whipped topping and garnish with cherries and blueberries. Serve.

OWEN VALLEY WINERY
SPENCER

Preston and Bonnie Leaderbrand were living in Illinois and perfectly happy, except for one thing: they wanted to be closer to their grandchildren Cody and Conner. That was the impetus that brought them to the small town of Spencer in Central Indiana. "Our son (Anthony) and daughter-in-law (Joanna) have been wine aficionados for a long time," said Bonnie. That started the germ of an idea. Once in Indiana, the Leaderbrands purchased forty acres and decided to plant a test plot of grapes to see the viability of opening a winery. The test grapes did well and vineyards were started, but a lot of work and decisions still needed to be done.

"We pooled all of our resources," explained Bonnie. "The winery building was a horse barn with dirt floors. While the grapes were growing we worked on the building, turning it into a tasting and production room." They started the grapes and process of building and licensure for a small farm winery in 2005, and Owen Valley Winery opened in June of 2011.

"We all started making wine in carboys in the basement," Bonnie went on. They concentrated on local fruit. The area is famous for persimmons and they've created wine with them. The port-style persimmon is aged in Maker's Mark bourbon barrels for an extra layer of flavor. It took a lot of wine experimentation and

winery work to see the roles that fit each person best. "Our daughter-in-law Joanna has the nose for whether a wine is fermenting right and how to finish the wines. Our son Anthony does all of the graphic arts for the labels." All of them took classes at Purdue. "Preston is the vineyard worker and I'm the manager of the tasting room," said Bonnie as she smiled proudly. "Our grandson Cody will be taking over soon. Connor is a student at I.U. studying business. He's learning how to do the tubes, which helps to keep the wine safe, tasting well, smelling well, and generally a good wine." They're delighted to have been involved in the start of something that will be handed down to future generations.

Owen Valley Winery
491 Timber Ridge Road
Spencer, IN 47460
812-828-0883

Tasting Room:
Owen Valley Winery at
  the Historic Tivoli Theatre
28 North Washington Street
Spencer, IN 47460
812-828-0883

Events: Yes, outdoor only;
  up to 100

Trail: Indiana Uplands Wine Trail

The Leaderbrands do their best to ensure that every need of visitors is met. "We make grab and go plates with local meats, Wisconsin cheeses, crackers, grapes, and chocolate," Bonnie said. "On band nights, a local establishment caters dinners with pulled pork BBQ and other specialties." Of course, they help visitors pick out wines to pair with the foods.

In addition to the winery, there is a tasting room nearby at the Historic Tivoli Theater. Opening on New Year's Eve in 1928, the theater had the grandeur of many show houses of the time that showed movies and had live stage performances. By the time it closed in 1999, it had suffered several fires and underwent many renovations. A group called Friends of Tivoli brought needed attention to the plight of the old theater, and persuaded preservation and landmark societies to help stop a scheduled 2005 demolition. In 2012, Cook Group Incorporation stepped in to sponsor the restoration, and the theater is once again open to the public. One very interesting aspect is the ceiling, which is a replica of the night sky the first night the theater opened on New Year's Eve, 1928. The Leaderbrands are happy to serve visitors at both locations.

"The people who come are part of what makes owning a winery so satisfying," Bonnie said. When people come to visit a winery, they're very involved in exploring the new tastes associated with wines in different regions and from different wineries. "Encouraging them to try a product we've worked so hard on and seeing their reactions is very gratifying." Whether you visit the Leaderbrands at the winery or Tivoli tasting room, just be sure to visit.

Wines

Old River Red

A blend of Barbera, Carignane, Petite Syrah, and Alicante Bouschet, this is a beautiful garnet wine that is smoky with black cherries and plum flavors. Pair with beef.

Crimson and Cream

A blend of Catawba, Niagara, and Cayuga grapes, this top-selling wine will delight you with ripe berry flavors. Pair this wine with seafood salad or light sandwiches.

Valley Red

An Indiana favorite, the concord grape makes for a delightfully sweet and smooth wine that reminds you of Grandma's fresh grape jelly. Drink cold or warm and add mulling spices.

Persimmon Heritage

Made from 100% local persimmons, this wine is delicately infused with pure cinnamon and vanilla, producing a light golden hue. Drink as an after-dinner aperitif or pair with apple pie with a slice of sharp cheddar on top.

Recipe

Persimmon Pudding

Although called pudding, this is more cake-like in texture

2 cups Owen Valley Persimmon wine
2 cups persimmon pulp
2 ½ cups sugar
2 cups all-purpose flour
2 tsp. baking powder
½ tsp. baking soda
2 eggs, beaten
½ tsp ground cinnamon
½ tsp vanilla extract
4 Tbl. Melted butter

In mixing bowl, stir together pulp, baking soda, sugar, and eggs. Mix well. Add flour, baking powder, cinnamon, vanilla, salt, wine, and melted butter. Stir. Turn oven to 325° and grease a 9x13 baking dish. Pour mix into dish and bake for an hour. The pudding will rise in the oven, but fall as it cools. That's what it's supposed to do. Cut and serve with a dollop of whipped cream sprinkled with cinnamon and sugar.

BUTLER WINERY & VINEYARDS
BLOOMINGTON

"We believe in Indiana grown"
– Jim and Susie Butler

Since opening in 1983, it could be debated that Jim and Susie Butler have done more to promote and expand the wine industry in Indiana than any other person. Butler Winery and Vineyards, located in the beautiful city of Bloomington, is the fourth oldest continuously operating winery in Indiana. "We're open every day of the year except Thanksgiving, Christmas, and New Year's Day," explained Jim. "When I opened, there were seven wineries total, but some of them were doing it as a hobby." The Butler's viewed the winery as a serious business from the start.

This can be seen in Jim's dedication to learning the wine industry. He started winemaking as a hobby, and then went to work for Bill Oliver Sr. at Oliver's Winery & Vineyards. The winemaker at the time was Bruce Zoecklein, who had a bachelor's of microbiology. He later acquired a master's in horticulture and a Ph.D. in food science and technology. Butler's degree is in limnology, the study of biological, chemical, and physical features of lakes and other fresh water. He joked that, "I took the algae out, put the yeast in and turned water into wine." When Zoecklein left, Butler took over as winemaker. He left there to open his own winery.

"I'd always been interested in chemistry," Butler explained. "Dad has a Ph.D. in organic chemistry." Jim's father is a story all by himself. Now 99 and living nearby, he has a computer and loves to do research in his field. As a boy, John saw Charles Lindberg on his triumphant tour of the U.S. after his solo flight to Europe. As a young man, John lived down the street from Orville Wright. Later in life, he consulted with the space program in Huntsville, Alabama where Wernher von Braun, credited with inventing the Saturn V rocket for the US space program, worked. John worked alongside his son and daughter-in-law at the beginning and still visits the winery.

Although Butler willingly took us through what he called his "40 year education of making wine," at many of the wineries we visited, the owners gave him kudos for expanding the wine industry in Indiana. Butler and his son John thoroughly researched the history of the wine industry in Indiana to write the book Indiana Wine; A History. Although written in 2001, the book is still popular today. "I planned to write a one page history," said Jim. "After 10 years of research, pre-internet, we wrote the book."

Along with running the winery; with Susie's help, being the winemaker, and writing the book, Jim also helped to set up the winery team at Purdue and pushed to establish the Indiana Uplands, an American Viticulture Area (AVA) in Indiana. To qualify as an AVA, an area has to be designated as a wine grape-growing region that is different from the surrounding area in regards to grape growing. This will give the wines in the AVA their own unique tastes. "The area from Bloomington to Louisville is a high plateau," explained Butler. Because of this, the glaciers couldn't go over it and the topography and soils remained the same."

Although it seems as if all of Butler's other pursuits for the wine industry would leave him little time to focus on wine, their Chambourcin Rosé has won gold at the 2nd largest wine competition in the country. Their dedication to the Indiana wine industry, growing and acquiring local grapes, and making great wines, are only a portion of what makes the experience at Butler Winery and Vineyards extra special. Come and sip the history soon.

Butler Winery & Vineyards
6200 East Robinson Road
Bloomington, IN 47408
812-332-6660

Tasting Rooms:
Butler Winery Chesterton
401 Broadway,
Chesterton, IN 46304
219-929-1400

Butler Winery "In Town"
1022 North College
 (15th and College)
Bloomington, IN 47404
812-339-7233

Events: Yes, small groups
 up to 50

Trail: Indiana Uplands Wine Trail

Wines

❧ Variant

A dry red blend of Chambourcin and Marquette wines aged in oak barrels. The lingering cherry aftertaste pairs well with walnut cake, tuna, or strawberries.

❧ Vineyard Rosé

A blend of Catawba, Concord, and Chambourcin give this wine its gorgeous pink color and fresh, grapy character. Enjoy with Asian cuisine or barbecue.

❧ Southshore White

Our newest semi-sweet wine is made from a blend of Seyval and our own Vidal grapes; it's light, fruity, and refreshing. Mix with some watermelon and cantaloupe for an extra special flavor.

❧ Cassis Noir

We've taken Black Currant wine and added grape brandy. Similar in style to a port, it pairs oh so well with dark chocolate and is excellent in sauces.

Recipe

Whipped Peach Shake

1 cup Butler's Peach Wine
1 15 oz. can peaches in heavy syrup
1 8 oz. tub frozen whipped topping (keep frozen)

Directions:
   Place all ingredients into blender, mix until smooth.
Pour into two tall glasses and serve immediately.

OLIVER WINERY & VINEYARDS
BLOOMINGTON

*"At Oliver Winery we connect people through wine,
and that's really the best part of our story."*
– The Oliver Family

While visitors are walking up to the entrance of Oliver Winery & Vineyards, they may get caught up in the beautiful gardens. Unusual plants, fountains, colorful trees, and multiple decks containing pergolas draped with grape vines, are truly a treat for the eye. Many visitors mill about and settle into shaded areas overlooking the pond. It's so entrancing they may forget to make it into the tasting room. We highly suggest you do not. Their wine is fantastic.

Oliver Winery started several years before opening day when Professor William Oliver, an Indiana University law professor, started making wine in his basement as a hobby. In 1920, when Prohibition started with the eighteenth amendment, people who lived an agricultural lifestyle dependent on grapes had to tear out most of their vines and find another cash crop. When Prohibition ended in 1933, many states did not encourage vineyards regrowth and many farmers

did not replant grapes, as they take about three years for the first good crop after planting, and another 1-2 for the first batch of wine. Many years later, when Professor Oliver's hobby got away from him, he was instrumental in bringing a small farm winery bill to legislation and getting it passed in 1971. In 1972, because of the bill, his was the first winery to open in Indiana since Prohibition. He started small with a selection of wines, but experimented with different grapes. When he created a light honey wine, Camelot Mead, their reputation began to grow quickly. Since then, Oliver's has become a popular showplace, visited by people from nearly every state and several countries.

In 1983, Professor Oliver's son Bill took over the winery. His focus became the visitor experience. He planted the gardens and trained employees on exceptional customer service, which is still emphasized today. By 1990, they were selling 25,000 cases a year. Bill has passed on the general manager mantle to Kathy Oliver and focuses on making wine and maintaining the vineyard.

Creekbend Vineyards, the vineyard that Oliver Winery maintains, is located on 54 ideally situated acres on a hilltop in Southern Indiana. Limestone soil that is well drained as well as long and warm summers and winters that do not get too cold to ruin the vines, allow many varieties of grapes the opportunity to ripen to perfection. Started in 1994, Oliver's aim with Creekbend Vineyards has carried out a commitment to produce great wines from Indiana-grown grapes. Visitors can tour the expansive vineyards, by appointment only. Oliver's also hosts a few special events each year in which they open up the vineyard to guests.

Another interesting and unique part of Oliver Winery and Vineyards is they are 100% employee owned through a stock ownership plan. This happened in 2006 and honored dedicated employees in a solid and concrete manner. They have a real stake in the winery and its success. It spurs them to do the best job possible, and this is seen by every visitor to the winery. Visit Oliver's Winery and Vineyard soon and experience the dedication.

Oliver Winery & Vineyards
200 E. Winery Road
Bloomington, IN 47404
812-876-5800

Events: Yes, up to 150

Trail: Indiana Uplands Wine Trail

Wines

☙ Pinot Grigio

Cool fermentation captures the delicate aromas of pear and citrus. This crisp wine works best with light seafood or fresh garden vegetables such as a cucumber and tomato salad.

☙ Creekbend Noir

A dry red featuring a blend of Marechal Foch Corot Noir. Aromas of black cherries alight in this fruit forward wine. Pair with roast duck or use in your favorite beef bourgeon recipe.

☙ Gewürztraminer

Delicate floral aromas with a zesty finish. A delicious match for spicy Asian or Latino dishes.

☙ Camelot Mead

Our classic honey wine expresses the delicate floral and citrus notes of orange blossom honey. Pairs well with salads and finger foods. Make a spritzer with a half glass of super-chilled mead and pour ginger ale, club soda, or lemon-lime soda until the glass is ¾ full. Place a slice of lime on top and serve immediately.

Pairing

We paired Oliver's Creekbend Noir wine with the recipe for Braised Short Ribs from Powers' Winery on page 211.

CEDAR CREEK WINERY & BREW CO.
MARTINSVILLE

The lovely and relaxed surroundings at Cedar Creek Winery and Brew Co., nestled in the countryside of Martinsville, Indiana, beckons to visitors as they come up the drive. Irises bloomed and hanging baskets overflowed with flowers in front of the structure, which was part cottage and part reminiscent of an old mill. This is to delineate the difference between the winery and the brewery. Nice inside and outside seating areas encourage visitors to linger awhile and the family who owns Cedar Creek welcomes you like old friends. Their winery dog, Cayuga, is excited to see guests too, but this laid-back Boxer isn't always really good at showing it.

Owners Larry and Donell Elsner, along with their family and friends, are determined, hard-working people. When the economy bottomed out, Larry's construction business was hit especially hard. He'd played around with making wine at home and had the idea that a winery might be a good idea. From the night he decided to pursue it, he focused on making the dream become reality. They bought the winery property in April of 2010, started construction in May, and the winery opened in the fall – nine short months after the thought first came to Larry.

The brewery was part of the original plan and is owned by the Elsner's son Bryce and his wife Jamie.

Bryce's formal title is manager and brew master. "We're open six days a week and I'm here seven," he smiled. Though running a winery and brewery requires a lot of work, Bryce didn't seem to mind that we interrupted his mowing to speak with him. This demonstrated to us another aspect that makes the winery a success; excellent customer service.

When asked about the name of Cedar Creek Winery, he explained, "There isn't a cedar tree on the place. Dad used to own Cedar Mill Builders and always thought the name added character to a business. He planned the buildings and wanted something that would look cool and have a lot of class." That they do.

A cedar barn sits on the property, with a small fenced pasture beside it. The pasture holds their pet goats Gertrude, Sally, and Betsy. A windmill slowly rotates with a soft breeze and a classic 1948 Chevy truck and antique wagon add an old world charm. Inside, the new and varied menu is a welcome addition, but the wine and microbrews are the stars at Cedar Creek Winery and Brew Co.

"Family and friends work both the tasting bar and the tap room, where people are often gathered around three deep," said Bryce. "When we have weddings we need even more help." Their wines include the big dry reds such as Cabernet Sauvignon and Pinot Noir, refreshing semi-dry wines such as Riesling and Malbec, a large selection of fruit wines and even an ice wine made with Cab Franc grapes. The micro-brewery offers a variety of ales, porters, and stouts. At Cedar Creek Winery and Brew Co. people come for the atmosphere, but stay for the excellent wine, customer service, and microbrews. Cheers!

Cedar Creek Winery & Brew C
3820 Leonard Road
Martinsville, IN 46151
765-342-9000

Tasting Room:
38 Franklin Street East
Franklin House 4
Nashville, IN 47448
812-988-1111

Events: Yes, outdoor, up to 175

Trail: Indy Wine Trail

Wines

❧ Aussie Red

This Shiraz is a versatile red wine with a hint of blackberry and fragrant spices. Pair with smoked meats and game or even a chocolate meringue pie with fresh raspberries.

❧ Sweet Inspiration

A red port with rich raspberry and chocolate flavors. A dessert all by itself.

❧ Royal Oak

This Chardonnay has a vanilla-oak structure that is very appealing. It pairs well with rich sauces such as Hollandaise and Béarnaise on grilled vegetables, steak, or salmon.

❧ Peach Paradise

Bursting with peach and apricot flavors, this wine adds a punch to sangria or peach cobbler. It pairs well with picnic foods and soft cheeses such as goat or brie.

Recipe

Chardon-YAY!

1 cup Cedar Creek Royal Oak Chardonnay
½ cup pineapple rum
½ cup pineapple juice
½ tsp vanilla extract
Fresh pineapple wedge for garnish

Directions:

Mix all ingredients in a pitcher. Divide evenly between two wine glasses and garnish with a pineapple wedge. Be sure to keep the ingredients around for this crowd pleaser.

BROWN COUNTY WINERY
NASHVILLE

"We want to make high quality grape and fruit wines with affordable prices."
– Dave and Cynthia Schrodt

When Dave and Cynthia Schrodt first opened Brown County Winery in 1985, there were a total of 19 wineries in Indiana, now there are nearly 90. "We were too poor to have our own garage," Dave joked. "We had to rent a garage to make wine." This vein of humor can be seen throughout the winery. Small signs with funny sayings are hanging all over and a new line of wines shares the name of a little burg close by, Chateau Gnaw Bone. In France, it is customary to put the chateau or castle on the label; the Chateau Gnaw Bone series has something completely different, but you'll have to visit to see what it is. They may like to joke around at Brown County Winery, but they are very serious when it comes to winemaking.

Since opening, they have won a number of awards including trophies, "Best of Class" several times, and close to one hundred and fifty medals for their wines. According to Brown County's website, "The Indy International Wine Competition is the largest scientifically organized and independent wine competition in the United States. This highly competitive contest draws entries from all over the world. In 2015, they received over 2,000 entries from 40 states and 11 countries." This competition is held in August every year and has a huge following with many thousands attending.

In 2000, the Schrodt's had some growing pains and decided to build a second winery building in Gnaw Bone, just outside of the town of Nashville. The beautifully landscaped log cabin structure has a wraparound porch, perfect for sitting and taking in the natural surroundings while sharing a picnic and bottle, or two, of wine with some friends.

The Schrodts make everything they sell. Customers really appreciate this as they have so many return visitors. "I really enjoy our customers who seek us out again and again," said Cynthia. "We learn their names and they become like old friends." Judging by the amount of cars in the parking lot, they have a lot of friends. Dave and Cynthia Schrodt invite you to stop in soon and become one of their friends too. "Our goal is to provide our customers with high quality, local wines, a relaxed atmosphere, and an enjoyable and educational experience." We guarantee you'll return.

Question: On Average, how many pounds of grapes does it take to make a bottle of wine?
Answer: About 2 ½ pounds.

Brown County Winery
4520 State Road 46 East
Nashville, IN 47448
812-988-6144

Tasting Room:
Corner of Main Street
 and Old School Way
Nashville, IN 47448
812-988-8646

Events: No

Trail: Indiana Uplands Wine Trail

Wines

> ❧ **Merlot**
> A dry red wine, oaky with soft tannins, enjoy it with lamb or your favorite sharp cheese and fruit.

> ❧ **Vista White**
> This slightly sweet white wine is made with a blend of hybrid and vinifera grapes. Enjoy a glass on a picnic or with lighter summer meals.

> ❧ **Old Barrel Port**
> (20% alcohol) barrel aged and smooth, enjoy this port-style wine with dessert or as a nightcap; it warms you all the way down.

> ❧ **Chateau Gnaw Bone Black Raspberry**
> (23% alcohol) this cordial pairs well with chocolate and cheesecake; it's the perfect finish to any day.

From the Winery

Chocolate Cocoa Balls

¼ cup Old Barrel Port or Chateau Gnaw Bone Black Raspberry
1 cup fine vanilla wafer crumbs
1 cup finely chopped pecans
1 cup confectioner's sugar
2 Tbls. Unsweetened cocoa powder
2 Tbls. light corn syrup
½ to 1 cup confectioner's sugar, sifted (for rolling) or granulated sugar, if you prefer

Directions:

Thoroughly combine vanilla wafer crumbs, pecans, confectioner's sugar, and cocoa. In a separate bowl, mix wine with the corn syrup. Stir liquid ingredients into dry mixture. Cover and chill for at least three hours. Sift confectioner's sugar, or pour granulated sugar, into wide bowl. Shape small bits of dough into balls and roll them in sugar. Store in refrigerator in tightly sealed container. These can be frozen for longer storage.

Photo by Kathy Woodhouse

SIMMONS WINERY
COLUMBUS

When you open the door to Simmons Winery, the first thing you notice is the delicious smell of brick oven pizzas baking. The next thing is the amount of people inside the building. Nearly every table was filled at lunchtime on the day we were there. "On Friday and Saturday nights," exclaimed Lauren Simmons, "there can be up to an hour wait for a table." It's definitely worth the wait.

Lauren is daughter of owners David and Brenda Simmons, who established the winery in 2000. A few years before, they'd planted vineyards with the idea to sell them to other wineries. Within a year, they were looking into what it took to open a winery. The Simmons opened the winery as an extension of their 150 year old farm that has been passed down through generations of the family. Currently, they've sold produce for over

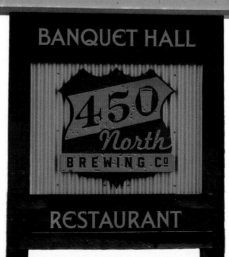

fifty years. The farm still produces many fruits and vegetables including melons, green beans, corn, pumpkins and squash to sell at farmer's markets. The winery is truly a family business, but also includes friends who have become family.

Tracy Fugate is the winery manager and joked about Jean Kelsay, Brenda Simmon's mother, who helps out at the winery with everything. "Don't ever make Grandma Jean mad," laughed Tracy, "and she'll be your best friend." The wonderful people who own and run the winery are just one of the things that make a visit here so special.

After working at the winery, brothers Aaron and Daron Simmons wanted to investigate what it would take to open a brewery in Indiana. Part of the rules included serving food and having separate bars for the wine and the beer.

172

The Simmons expanded the winery to include a brick oven for pizzas, plus a selection of sandwiches, salads, appetizers, and pastas, and opened 450 Brewing Company in 2012. There are a large selection of popular brews including Farmer's Daughter, with fruity and spicy notes, plus a crisp finish, and Beam Me Up Scotty, a Scottish-style ale with a deep color and flavors of malt and roasted hops. The Gnarly Grove Cidery was started in 2014. It is quickly expanding its selections which include LegendBerry, which is a pressed apple cider mixed with blackberries, raspberries, and blueberries, and Dry-Hopped Cider, which is made with five kinds of hops and bursts with green apple flavor. Although the winery, brewery, cidery, and restaurant may seem like the Simmons have a lot on their plate, their hope is to grow even more.

In September 2016, the Simmons and two other family members opened Riverfront Tap Room in Shelbyville, Indiana. "On October 1st we will be the first place in the US to hold a beer festival in a corn maze," said Lauren. Luckily, there is someone to help keep their feet on the ground. "My dad does everything connected with the farm," Lauren explained. "He's the voice of reason around here. We can all get crazy ideas, and he brings us back down to earth." Lauren's father, David, has found a calm counterpart in his wife Brenda. "Mom does a lot with weddings and other events in the banquet hall and takes care of the memorial garden."

The garden is a tribute to many family members and pets who have passed on. The lovely plants and structures afford visitors a place to sit in natural surroundings and absorb the beauty and atmosphere of the farm. It's a place to slow down, visit, and enjoy each other's company with a glass or two of wine. Cheers!

Simmons Winery
8111 East 450 North,
Columbus, IN 47203
812-546-0091

Events: Yes, indoors up to 225; outdoors up to 75

Wines

❧ Chambourcin

This deep colored, aromatic wine with full-fruit taste balanced with mild acidity. It would pair well with dark chocolate, grilled salmon, or lamb.

❧ Vidal Blanc

The crisp beginning of this wine leads to a smooth, full-grape finish. It pares well with vegetarian dishes, fruit and cheese platters, shellfish, and chicken.

❧ Riesling

The apple and pear tastes of this wine end on a satisfying floral note. This wine goes especially well with a red snapper with poblano peppers and a squeeze of fresh lime.

❧ Cranberry Apple

Both tart and not too sweet, this satisfying wine would work well warmed with a cinnamon stick and sprinkle of cloves.

From the Winery

Simmons Blackberry Wine Cake

Cake:
¼ cup Simmons Blackberry Wine
1 box of white cake mix with pudding
1 small package of blackberry or raspberry gelatin
¾ cup vegetable oil (we find olive oil doesn't taste as good in baked goods as other oils)
½ cup milk
4 eggs
1 cup fresh or frozen blackberries
1 cup flaked coconut
1 cup chopped nuts

Icing:
⅛ cup Simmons Blackberry Wine
½ cup of butter, softened
4 ½ cups powdered sugar
Dash of milk
½ cup blackberries
½ cup coconut
½ cup pecans

In mixing bowl, combine cake mix, gelatin, wine, oil, and milk. Mix until blended. Add eggs one at a time, mixing after each one. Fold in blackberries, coconut, and pecans. Pour into three greased 9 inch pans. Bake at 350° for 25-30 minutes. Cool.

For icing, in mixer or with hand mixer in large bowl, beat together butter and powdered sugar. Add wine, milk, and berries and mix well. Next, add the coconut and pecans. If it seems too thin for spreading, add powdered sugar a tablespoon at a time. If it's too thin, add wine a teaspoon at a time.

SALT CREEK WINERY
FREETOWN

"Using the finest ingredients, we strive to produce quality wines that are minimally processed."
– Adrian and Nichole Lee

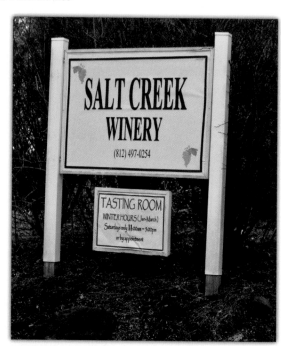

As visitors drive up to the lovely tasting room at Salt Creek Winery, they are greeted by Cassie, a border collie who is the winery dog. She used to be a sheep dog, but she lost her job when winery owners Adrian and Nichole Lee sold the sheep. When coming through the immense wooden door, people are greeted warmly by both the hosts and other guests. This is a winery that feels like a warm gathering of friends from hello to goodbye.

Adrian Lee emigrated from England at 16, and one can still hear a slight English accent when speaking with him. "My father had a job offer that was supposed to last for three years." It stretched into five and when he was offered a permanent job, America became their home. Although a winery owner now, that was never in their original plans.

"I started home brewing beer, and several years ago; Nichole asked me to try wine." Although generations of Adrian's family had made wines, he'd never attempted it himself. It turned out well. "When friends wanted to buy it, I applied for a license. Originally, I just wanted to sell enough to pay for supplies," Lee explained. Friends shared it with other friends and his sales took off. Lee started going to farmer's markets and expanding his operation. In 2003, the Lees bought some land bordering Hoosier National Forest and built a home. Several years later,

they had the Amish build the outside of their tasting room and finished the inside themselves. The winery opened in 2012.

They specialize in what they call "Country Style Wine", meaning the wine is made from grapes and berries that traditionally grow in the rolling hills

176

close to their Southern Indiana home. "Catawba is our best seller," said Nichole.

"Our 100% fruit wines are fermented as if they were grapes and are not back sweetened with fruit juice or concentrate," Adrian exclaimed. "When fermented, each fruit develops its own unique character, much like a grape, and we prefer to allow this character to be dominant in the flavor of the wine and not to be masked by the flavor of unfermented juice." What this does is produce a pure fruit taste that lasts all the way through to the finish. "100% juice takes on the flavor of the fruit rather than the juice."

Nichole's favorite part of owning a winery is getting to interact with a lot of people, which she loves. "We get requests for different types of wine and we try to keep something here for everyone. We're working on a black currant, set to come out later this year, which we expect to be very popular."

For Adrian, it's the process of winemaking and creating new wines that hold his interest the most. "We strive to produce quality wines that are minimally processed," he said. "We believe mechanical filtering and chemical fining take some of the quality out of wine, so we only do it when necessary for shelf life."

Adrian retired in May of 2016, but Nichole still works full-time at a pharmaceutical company. Despite being so busy, within five years they see themselves opening another tasting room and hiring a full-time wine maker.

Visit Salt Creek Winery and have a talk with the Lees. Bring a picnic lunch or have one of their cheese plates and sit at one of the tables in the back where the land seems to stretch for miles. Sip some of the best country wines you've probably ever tasted, and let any stress slide away like a fall sunset.

Salt Creek Winery
7603 West CR 925 North
Freetown, IN 47235
812-497-0254

**Tasting Room and
 Salt Creek Winery Loft**
26 N. Honeysuckle Lane
Nashville, IN 47448
812-497-0254

Events: No

Wines

❧ Merlot

This oaked dry contains hints of cherry and currant. It pairs well with smoked meats, roasted vegetables, and spicy jambalayas.

❧ Classic White

A dry white made with choice grapes, this floral and fruity wine is best served chilled. Serve with fresh baked bread and spicy salami, a light grilled fish, or your favorite salad.

❧ Blush

This award winner is crisp and refreshing. Pair with Mexican dishes, a roasted chicken, or even pretzels.

❧ Peach

Like eating a fresh slice of peach pie, this wine is great to pair with fruit desserts, crab cakes, or fragrant cheeses such as goat or bleu. Also a great wine to serve at a bonfire.

From the Winery

Salt Creek Port-Style Merlot Cheese Ball

¼ cup Salt Creek Port-Style Merlot (up to ½ cup can be used if desired)
¼ cup butter, at room temperature
16 ounces sharp cheddar cheese, grated
8 ounces cream cheese at room temperature
1 cup walnuts, chopped

Directions:

In a food processor, combine cheddar cheese and cream cheese. Pulse the food processor on and off until the two are just mixed. Put this cheese mixture into a bowl. In the food processor, process butter until smooth. While the machine is running, pour in small amounts of wine, processing steadily until well mixed. Add the wine/butter mixture to the cheese mixture. Mix together with a spoon. Form cheese into a ball, roll in chopped walnuts, wrap in plastic wrap and refrigerate. Serve with crackers.

CHATEAU DE PIQUE WINERY & VINEYARD

SEYMOUR

The sheer size of this winery is apt to make visitors stop and stare. Acres of vineyards roll along the slope of the landscape toward a massive stone arch. The area around the arch consists of amphitheater-like seating, beautiful landscaping and a reflecting pool. The lovely surroundings is only one of the many reasons to visit this South Central Indiana winery situated in Seymour.

Visitors might notice white roses growing at the beginning of many of the rows of grapes. Some people believe this is to draw in bees to help pollinate the

plants, but this isn't necessarily true. One reason is that roses bloom too late to draw in bees that would pollinate the grapes and another, very important reason this information has shown to not be completely accurate is that grape vines are self-pollinating. This means that the vines produce both male and female flowers, and the transfer of pollen happens naturally. However, there is a very important reason you'll often see roses planted at vineyards.

Roses and grape vines are susceptible to many of the same types of diseases, especially a certain type of mildew, which is common to the area. If rose leaves start showing a gray, powdery substance, the vines may be sprayed with Sulphur, which will not cure the disease, but will prevent it. Many of the roses at Chateau De Pique are white, to symbolize a sweet tradition owner Gregg Pardieck started when he gave his wife a dozen red roses upon the birth of their son and included one white rose to symbolize him. Every year on his birthday, Pardieck presents his son one white rose.

**Chateau De Pique Winery
& Vineyard**
6361 North County Road
760 East
Seymour, IN 47274
812-522-9296

Tasting Room:
6725 East 82nd Street
Indianapolis, IN 46250
317-578-7413

Events: Yes, indoor up to 100,
outdoor up to 450

Also featured within the eighty acres that encompass Chateau De Pique Winery and Vineyard is a beautiful, lovingly restored 19th century barn that houses the tasting room. Designed to be warm and inviting, the seating area beckons visitors with its comfortable chairs and intimate lighting. Outside, the quilt square painting on the barn continues the cozy feeling as the beautiful landscaping surrounds visitors. In the spring, hundreds of lilies bob in the breeze as guests walk the trails around the property. The upper floor sports a cavernous ceiling and the room is set up to perform weddings. It's a beautiful space for a special day.

Another feature of the winery is, of course, the wine. "We produce about 3,800 gallons of wine a year." With more than twenty varieties, there's something for every palate. Several wines, including their Estate Vignoles, Cabernet Franc, Chardonel, and Blackberry, have garnered medals at the Indy International Wine Competition. There are many oaked and unoaked selections, as well as wines made with other fruits and berries. Their dry Riesling is a personal favorite and their Peach Bum and Bravo Blueberry were both sold out. In addition to the winery, Chateau De Pique offers visitors the choice of beer in their microbrewery called CdP Brewery. Whatever type of adventure visitors may be looking for, they can find it at Chateau De Pique. Bring some food and friends and taste the country atmosphere.

> *I love everything that's old – old friends,
> old times, old manners, old books, old wine.*
> – Oliver Goldsmith

Wines

Oaked Chardonel

Light, crisp beginning with a slight toasted pine nut and buttery finish. Pair with rich fish such as salmon in a basil cream sauce, starch dishes, and crusty breads.

Estate Vignoles

This estate grown wine has a peach and floral nose and piquant, citrusy body with a lingering apricot finish. Pair it with soft cheeses such as goat, bleu, or feta.

Love Potion No. Wine

A combination of sweet, vibrant cherry with a tart finish. This well-balanced wine pairs with chocolate meringue pie, or a strawberry and feta green salad.

Fifty Shades of Red

Racy lemon tartness, red berries, and honey highlight this Steuben-Vignoles blended wine. Interesting for a spritzer with ginger ale and pineapple juice.

Recipe

Perfect Lemony

This is such a great flavor combination, you'll wonder why you haven't put them together before.

¼ cup Chateau De Pique Blackberry Port, chilled
1 scoop of lemon sherbet or sorbet
Blackberries for garnish

Place sherbet or sorbet in bowl, pour port over top and garnish with blackberries.

STREAM CLIFF HERB FARM TEAROOM & WINERY
COMMISKEY

*"Celebrate gardening, delicious food, delightful wine,
and antiques at one of the nation's oldest herb farms."*
– The Manning Family

It will be hard in a short article to describe all of the things that make this a must-visit winery. We came to the winery-gardens-herb farm-restaurant on a Wednesday afternoon, thinking there wouldn't be as many people as there are on the weekends. The parking lot was full and people were pulling red wagons to pick out plants, eating at the restaurant, and enjoying the many tables set up in the shade, as well as sampling their fabulous wines.

During the Revolutionary War (1775-1783), the new country of America did not have money to pay soldiers who fought for the cause, but they did have plenty of one thing—land. Land grants were given to soldiers as payment for their services and in 1821, James Harmon came to the land granted to his father. This would eventually become Stream Cliff Herb Farm Tearoom and Winery. Harmon never married, and after his death soon after Morgan's Raiders came through during the Civil War (1861-1865), he left his property to the church. This is where the first members of the Manning family purchased the farm and began the traditions now passed down to seven generations. Betty Manning is matriarch of the farm and has overseen its extensive growth.

The beautiful gardens are laid out like quilt blocks to honor a grandmother who loved to quilt and garden as both a necessity and a creative outlet. The original home built by James Harmon is still standing on the property. It took Harmon several years to build the house, as he built it all himself, even making and baking all of the bricks by hand. The home and gardens are just one part of the story of the farm though, as the restaurant, winery, and antique shop also capture people's attention.

"We have regulars who come once or twice a week," said Betty's son Greg. "We've been open for busi-

Stream Cliff Herb Farm
  Tearoom & Winery
8225 South County Road 90 W
Commiskey, IN 47227
812-346-5859

Events: Yes, outdoor, up to 125

Trail: Indiana Wine Trail

ness for 35 years and always try to do a little something more every year." A little something is quite an understatement.

A former greenhouse on the property was converted to the restaurant, Twigs and Sprigs. Each table is inviting, set up with unique vases and colorful flowers. The restaurant utilizes every aspect of the farm, using herbs from the gardens for every item on the menu and any fresh produce when it's in season. Their selection of burgers, sandwiches, salads, and desserts are served with an edible flower and each has a suggested wine pairing. Do not skip eating at the restaurant while there. In addition to daily lunch, they host cooking classes and special, reservation only, candlelight dinners several times a year.

The winery harkens back to the blacksmith shop it used to house. The wines are named after horses or have horse themes. "Our heartfelt desire is that every time a visitor comes they have a delightful experience." There is extra seating in the winery and this is the space used for autumn lunches and the Candlelight Dinners. Their handcrafted wines include favorites such as Merlot and Chardonnay, as well as wines not often seen such as cranberry and black currant. In addition, they have a Christmas Wine, only available from October to December. Most of the time, visitors may choose between eighteen to twenty different types of wine to taste.

Looking at the list of events happening at Stream Cliff Farms, there is something new to do or enjoy nearly every day from April through December. Come and join in a class, listen to a band, or just sit and take in the beautiful surroundings, but whatever you do, you can't miss this gem in Southeast Indiana.

Wines

❧ Iron Hand

This wonderful, dry red Cabernet Sauvignon is complex as well as smooth. The winemaker's favorite, it's delicious with rosemary seasoned meals.

❧ Old Bo

Named after our favorite red horse, this dry and smooth wine is the perfect companion to red meat meals or dishes using thyme. Add it to your favorite steak sauce, too.

❧ My Dolly

This dry, white Chardonnay wine with a hint of oak pairs well with Alfredo sauces and dishes made with dill.

❧ Bareback

This pleasantly sweet blush wine with a beautiful color adds delight to any picnic, summer party, or wine punch.

Recipe

We like to pair everyday food with favorite wines. Stream Cliff recommends pairing grilled hamburgers with their concord wine. When we cook burgers, we like to mix a little of the wine, about ¼ cup per pound. In addition, ground beef will lose some juice if handled too much. Mix in a dry packet of ranch or Italian dressing, or an onion soup mix with the wine, then add to the ground beef and mix just until blended. Make loose patties and grill until desired doneness.

While visiting Stream Cliff Herb Farm, Tearoom, & Winery, be sure to try their blackberry cobbler. Tastes just like Grandma's.

MADISON VINEYARDS ESTATE WINERY
MADISON

"To Friends, To Family, and To the Good Earth!"
– Sandy and Steve Palmer

Making good, home grown wine is a long process, about five years from the first planting to the first production of wine. For Sandy and Steve Palmer, the journey from first making wine to opening a winery took quite a bit longer. "I always blame opening a winery on the wine kit I gave Steve for our first Christmas together," explained Sandy. All through the moves from that small apartment to a home with a basement, Steve continued making wine. He also joined wine clubs and tasting clubs to gain more knowledge.

"In 1975," Steve said. "We bought some land and planted a vineyard. We sold most of the grapes to other wineries, but I kept what I felt was the best to make my wine." The passion for wine making continued and grew, but so did the Palmers family. They sold the vineyard in the early '80s, always knowing they would return to grape growing when things slowed down a bit.

In 1994, the Palmers searched for just the right piece of land. "We wanted a site with well-drained soil and south-facing slopes. It would have to be close to a highway with a tourist area and have a bridge across the river," Steve Palmer explained. They found this perfect spot at the top of a hill in Madison. "The spot where the bed & breakfast sits used to be where the farmhouse was. The tornado of 1974 took it down and the woman who lived there had the house rebuilt close by. She lived in the new house one night, and then moved into the small cottage over there." She didn't like being in that big house all alone. Mr.

Madison Vineyards Estate
  Winery Bed & Breakfast
1456 E. 400 North
Madison, IN 47250
888-473-6500
812-273-6500

Events:

Trail: Indiana Wine Trail

Palmer pointed to a small yellow house next to the bed and breakfast. The bed and breakfast, built in 2006, has four guest rooms, plus there are two private cottages available. The decks of both the winery and the bed and breakfast afford fabulous views of the sun going down. Since the winery has no lights around it, the stars appear bright and plentiful, and it's a perfect spot to watch a meteor shower.

Madison Vineyards Estate Winery has gained national recognition, being featured as a "Top Spot" in Madison in the pages of Midwest Living Magazine. The 37 acre winery prides itself on growing all of their own grapes, earning their estate status. The Palmers take pride in their award winning wines. Their best seller, "Black Dog" won the prestigious "Best Sweet Wine in Indiana" at the Indy International Wine Competition. Their Ba-Da-Bing! Bianco is a dry red wine styled after wines from Central Italy.

Madison Vineyards is known for a variety of events, but their most popular are the Twilight Tasting Dinners, held once a month from February to October. Wine is meant to be served with food and the Palmers pair wines with four or five course dinners. Reservations are required and these fill up fast. Another thing that is included in these dinners is the spectacular sunset seen from the deck of the winery. Raise a glass as the last rays slip between the layers of night, and toast to friends, family, and the good earth. Cheers!

Wines

Ba-Da-Bing! "Rosso"

A dry red styled after the wines of Central Italy, this 100% estate blended wine is fruity and intense. Add this to or with your favorite soups and shellfish dishes.

Mousseux Mystique

A sparkling wine, similar to champagne, made from estate grown Niagara grapes. Wonderful with a rich plate of cheeses like goat and bleu or a dessert.

Rosato

A slightly sweet and spicy rosé wine with hints of berries. Serve at an outdoor dinner with grilled vegetables and an olive salad with basil, oregano, and garlic.

Black Dog

Madison Vineyards bestseller is this sweet red with hints of cherry. Voted "Best Sweet Wine in Indiana" at the Indiana Wine Fair.

Wine Pairing

Madison Vineyards creates the Ba-Da-Bing wine in both red (rosso) and white (bianco) varieties. We paired the Ba-Da-Bing Bianco with the Settlers Pride Turkey Casserole from Indian Trail Wines on page 71.

LANTHIER WINERY
MADISON

"A far away feeling, close enough to taste"
– Tami Hagemier

When you create a winery in a house with parts of it built in the 1700s, an original resident or two may still be around. "While we were restoring the winery," said winery co-owner Tami Hagemier, "someone stopped by to ask about the elderly lady who lived in the little red house and tended the garden." Her eyes widened as she explained. "There were holes in the floors of the house, part of the roof had caved in; no one could live there." Hagemier didn't think much about it, until it kept happening. "Finally I told them, 'if you see her again, tell her to pull some weeds because she's not pulling her weight around here.'"

"Before the winery," Hagermier added, "the property had quite a colorful past. Railroad workers created a trading post and depot exchange where more than items were 'exchanged.'" Although started for trading purposes, the depot became a well-known bordello. "The gardens were once a whole subdivision of shotgun houses. Later, it became a scrapyard and people from the town still remember bringing rubber tires and paper there during World War II."

In 1990, Chris Lanthier, Cellar Master, and his soon-to-be bride Tami Hagemier, Master Gardener, saw the beauty and history of the buildings and property through the mountains of metal, cardboard, and glass left when the scrapyard closed in the late 1970s. "We liked the European feel of it all," Hagemier explained. "The thick stone walls, stepping down into

the tasting room feels like stepping into a faraway place." She created the French country-style gardens to continue this Old World European feel outdoors.

During the cleanup, they saved some of the more interesting scraps and added them as garden sculptures—a railcar spring and railroad gear are just two examples. It took four years of cleaning, restoring and gardening to get the property ready. In September of 1994, Lanthier Winery first opened its doors with ten different wine varieties. Today, visitors have sixteen choices, plus three holiday wines. "We heat the Rudolph Red with a bag of mulling spices made especially for us," Hagemier exclaimed. "It tastes just like you think Christmas should taste." Free samples are offered during the kick-off weekend of one of Madison's most popular tourist attractions—Festival of Trees.

With more than 105 custom designed trees, Lanthier Winery becomes a shimmering forest from the end of November to the first of January each year. The display is different every time and the celebration is designated as a state attraction. It is the largest attended free event in the region. Families are welcomed, but children must be accompanied by an adult. Although this event is mainly inside, many of Lanthier's events involve their expansive gardens.

During the Spring Celebration Festival, visitors can meander through the nation's only interactive outdoor "Garden of Art." A small sampling bag is given so that visitors may freely take some of the flowers as they get down and dirty to help divide the extensive collection of bulbs. If guests would like more bulbs, a larger bag is available for a small donation to America in Bloom, which helps to plant gardens in many communities across the nation.

The giving spirit of the people at Lanthier can be seen in many ways, including their rehabilitation program. "We take young birds and animals that have been abandoned or orphaned," Hagemier pointed out. I can only imagine what people think when they pass by and see me with a baby bird on my head trying to teach them how to fly."

With gardens, hospitality, history, and entertaining stories being just a few of the many wonderful and interesting reasons to visit Lanthier Winery, it may slip guests' minds to sample the wine. We heartily suggest you do not forget. It's delicious.

Lanthier Winery
123 Mill St.
Madison, IN 47250
812-800-41-WINES
812-273-2409

Events: Yes Indoor seating, up to 40; Outdoor seating, up to 350

Trail: Indiana Wine Trail

Wines

❧ **Chambourcin**
Well suited for a wide variety of foods, this well-balanced wine is a nod to Mr. Lanthier, an important resident of the 1800s. Serve with a ham dinner or pasta and red sauce with Italian sausage.

❧ **Traminette**
Often called the grape of Indiana for its prominence in the state, this slightly fruity wine pairs well with a savory turkey and dressing dish.

❧ **Chautauquablumchen**
Meaning "Gathering of the Blossoms," this semi-sweet white made with Catawba grapes is a wonderful addition to an appetizer party.

❧ **Blackberry Social**
Sweet and light, this flavorful wine is great to sip with a few frozen raspberries and peach slices, or pair with a fruit salad.

Recipe

Traminette Pasta Salad

Vinaigrette:
½ cup Lanthier Winery Traminette
3 garlic cloves, minced
1 tsp. chopped fresh oregano
1 Tbl. chopped fresh basil
½ tsp. dried marjoram
3 Tbl. lemon juice
¾ cup extra virgin olive oil

Salt and freshly ground black pepper, to taste.

Place wine in saucepan on stovetop, whisk in all other ingredients and heat just to boil. Allow to cool. This helps to better incorporate all of the flavors.

Pasta:
1 pound small pasta shells, cooked according to package instructions and cooled
1 quart cherry tomatoes, halved
1 cup diced seedless cucumber
1 14.5 oz. can garbanzo beans, rinsed and drained
1 small can sliced Kalamata olives, drained
¾ cup crumbled feta cheese

Combine all ingredients in large bowl and toss with cooled vinaigrette. Season with salt and pepper. Serve with more Lanthier Traminette.

THOMAS FAMILY WINERY
MADISON

"Wines and ciders in the Welsh tradition"
– Steve Thomas

Steve Thomas swept his arm in an arc as he showed us his massive brick oven. "It's modeled after a late 17th century side flue Scotch oven in Llynon, Wales." The keystone at the top has a large capital V honoring Vesta, the goddess of home and hearth. "Vesta was also my great-grandmother's name." Thomas serves the fine bread baked in the oven to patrons as they taste his ciders and wines. "During the busiest times, we make eight dozen loaves a week." In addition, Thomas offers period catering, often delivering foods cooked and eaten in the style of that time frame to Revolutionary and Civil War reenactments.

Everything about the Thomas Family Winery has an old world feel. This is not surprising in a town with 133 blocks designated as a historic district. Many of the buildings and homes in Madison, Indiana were built when the town became an important shipping port in the early 1800s. When it was built, the railroad was the largest one in the state, larger even than the one at the capital in Indianapolis. The 1850s' building that houses the winery was originally a stable and carriage house. Steve Thomas makes only traditional wines, ciders, and breads in the old world style. With its old-fashioned games, brick walls, and wood burning cook stove, stepping through the doors at the Thomas Family Winery is entering another time period.

"I'm a third generation winemaker," Steve explained. "My grandfather taught my father how to make wine and hard ciders in the Welsh tradition. This means it's dry with an edge. You have to use the right type of craggy little apples to get the right flavors." Thomas was quick to give credit to others who helped to make Thomas Family Winery a success. "I had other good consultants and teachers along the way. Dick Vine was Indiana's first enologist and I received no short help from him."

An enologist is someone who has training in the chemistry and biology of wine. He or she analyzes all factors that go into wine and helps the wine maker to make better cider and wine. This is no small task as it involves fermentation, correcting problems, helping with blending decisions, and advising on all the equipment, supplies, and sanitation necessary to produce wine. The current enologist for Indiana at Purdue University is Christian Butzke.

To help with the old world feel at Thomas Family Winery, several photographs of the historic building through the years, adorn one wall. Thomas knows the entire history. "First it was a carriage house and stable, then a service station, next a bus station, The White Star Line. Before becoming a winery, the building had always centered around transportation of some kind." Although Thomas is very serious about his ciders, wines, and breads, he also hosts several fun and different events at the winery.

There's a toga party every summer, he holds Obscure Neil Young Nights; anyone can play and sing, they just have to sing a little known Neil Young song, and one weekend each April, he hosts a Hot Luck and Fiery Foods Marketplace. "There are cooking contests and tastings and people set up their wares on Saturday and Sunday," Thomas explained.

Whether visitors come for the wine and ciders, food, or entertainment, they fill up Thomas Family Winery to overflowing almost any weekend. Steve and Elizabeth Thomas invite you to come and join them.

Thomas Family Winery
208 E. Second St.
Madison, IN 47250
812-273-3755
800-948-8466

Trail: Indiana Wine Trail

Wines

⚜ Gale's Hard Cider
Tangy, strong and dry, this fermented like ale cider is wonderful to pair with spicy or curried dishes.

⚜ Sauvignon Blanc
Classic flavors of fig, peaches and tropical fruit with mint and tea finish, this is a versatile wine to serve with a shrimp salad or blackened fish dishes.

⚜ Sangria Rosé
The light and fruity version of the traditional Spanish drink, citrus zest adds a special zing. Perfect with the winery's bread and cheeses.

⚜ Dance Monkey Rougeon'
Rich Beaujolais flavors of cherry, strawberry, and floral notes, this wine is perfect to serve with sausages, grilled or roasted chicken and vegetables.

⚜ Native American Blush
A blend of Niagara and Concord grapes, this wine has hints of watermelon and peach. A porch sipping wine or pair with a salad filled with grilled fruits and cheeses.

Recipe

Dance Monkey Rougeon' Mulled Wine

1 bottle of Thomas Family Dance Monkey Rougeon'
4 cups apple cider
4 oranges
½ cup honey
4 cinnamon sticks
½ tsp. ground cloves

Directions:

Zest and juice one orange and slice the other three in thin slices. Heat the wine, cider, honey, cinnamon sticks and cloves to a boil. Reduce heat and simmer for ten minutes. Serve warm garnished with orange slices.

THE RIDGE WINERY TASTING ROOM
VEVAY

"Best winery by a dam site"
– Greg Pavy

The Ridge Winery Tasting Room located at 11048 E State Road 156, Vevay Indiana is a unique wine and gift shop that sits on one of the prettiest sites you're likely to find anywhere. Within view of the Markland Dam, the partially covered deck affords expansive views of the Ohio River and Kentucky hillsides. A special barrel-aged grape blend, "Dam View Red," is a popular wine choice of customers. Visitors love to sit and soak it all in while enjoying their favorite wine and cheese plate. The Ridge Winery Tasting Room under The Ridge Winery second location permit is operated by Greg and Traci Pavy. Opening in 2004, Greg and Traci Pavy are a phenomenal part of The Ridge Winery, keeping the shop open seven days a week for over twelve years.

The Ridge Farm Winery production area is located on the Demaree Family farm Northwest of Vevay, Indiana. In 1989, Tom Demaree decided to turn his passion into a business and began what became a five year process of starting a winery. With assistance from family and friends, he has seen his vision become a reality. Tom's twenty-five years' experience at Schenley Distillery, as well as making his own homemade wine, became a valuable asset along the way to opening a winery.

In 1995, The Ridge Winery opened with only three wines; Concord, Blush, and Blackberry. Now they produce a variety of seventeen wines using blends of fruits and select grapes. Tom Demaree's current title is "Winemaker and Distributor," while Jane Demaree is currently the owner of The Ridge Winery.

The Ridge Winery has a reputation for producing award winning wines. Jane said, "In 2015, The Ridge Winery entered three of their favorite wines in the prestigious Indiana International Wine Competition with over 2,000 entries from forty states and several countries." The Ridge Winery brought home three medals; bronze for their Riesling, silver for their BlackJack and gold for their Shiraz. 2015 was a very big year for both Tom and Jane Demaree and The Ridge Winery. Tom and Jane celebrated their 50th wedding anniversary and The Ridge Winery celebrated its 20th anniversary.

Tom's latest productions are wines aged in select Kentucky bourbon barrels. "We currently have three barrel-aged wines available," Jane said, "and they are becoming very popular with our customers."

Vevay, Indiana, population 1,681, a town in Switzerland County, was the chosen spot for John James DuFour (1802-1827) to continue his importance to the history of the wine industry, by planting his second commercial vineyard in America and the first successful commercial winery. He first attempted a winery in Kentucky, but it did not thrive. When a killing frost killed all of the vines in May of 1809, DuFour and his family moved to the Swiss immigrant community of Vevay. DuFour spent the rest of his days there and his grave site is in a small, private family cemetery nearby. Switzerland County Indiana is the birthplace of America's first successful commercial winery.

The Ridge Winery is one of the seven participating wineries on the Indiana Wine Trail. (www.indianawinetrail.com) They host a variety of events throughout the year including the Fall Haul in November which pairs food and wines and draws bigger crowds each year.

Niece and nephew, Traci and Greg Pavy are in charge of the day to day operation at The Ridge Winery Tasting Room, where visitors can taste all of the wonderful selections produced at The Ridge Winery. The Pavy's and Demarees invite all to come and share their space, their wines, and their generosity. We guarantee visitors will return again and again.

The Ridge Winery Tasting Room
11048 E. Hwy 156
Vevay, IN 47043
Ph: 812-427-3380
Cell: 812-599-3473
www.theridgewinery.com

Events: Outdoor seating 75, indoor seating 40

Trail: Indiana Wine Trail

Wines

Syrah/Shiraz

This semi-dry red is smooth and pleasing to the palate with just a hint of peppery flavor on the finish. Very good paired with smoked meats, lamb, or thick beef stew.

RuralCool-American Riesling

This crisp white has flavors of apple and melon. Light and fruity, this is the perfect wine for a white sangria. It also pairs well with fish such as salmon or snapper, or salads.

Dam View Red

This red blend is aged in bourbon barrels for a special flavor. Subtle hints of the bourbon and oak create interesting notes and smooth flavors. Adding this wine to a roast or steak will enhance their flavors. Pair it with barbecued meats, potatoes au gratin, and vegetables seasoned with ham or bacon.

Country Rosé

A Catawba grape blend with a pleasant aroma and taste. This is a good one to sip chilled or pair with appetizers for a cocktail party.

Black Jack

This winemaker's special blend of apple and blackberry wine is a unique flavor sensation. Great to sip or pair with a cheese and fruit plate.

From the Winery

The Ridge Winery Blackberry Wine Cobbler

(This recipe may be halved for a smaller cobbler)

½ cup of Ridge Winery Blackberry Wine
Pastry dough for a double crust
36-48 oz. of frozen or fresh berries (blackberries/raspberries/blueberries or a mixture is tasty. Use as many as needed to fill the pie crust)
¼ cup melted butter or margarine
4 Tbls. flour, sifted
3 to 4 cups of sugar, or Splenda® Sweetener to your taste; less will give the cobbler a tart taste

Directions:

Tip: Use a deep baking dish to avoid the fruit juice boiling over while cooking.

Pre-heat oven to 350°. In a 33x23 baking dish for a large or 13x9 for a small cobbler, place one crust in bottom of pan and then add berries on top of the crust. Pour melted butter or margarine over berries. Sprinkle sifted flour and sugar or Splenda® over berries and pour wine over the top. Cover berries with second pie crust. Bake until top of crust is golden brown. Serve warm or cool with a scoop of French vanilla ice cream.

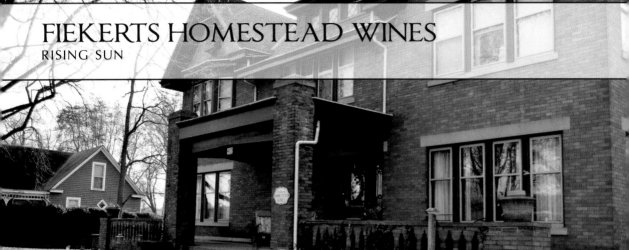

FIEKERTS HOMESTEAD WINES
RISING SUN

"Let us share some wine with you; after all, wine is about celebration."
– Ken and Vickie Fiekert

Fiekerts has a unique business model that includes using the finest juice, grapes and berries from nearby and from the best regions for the fruit all over the world. They carefully monitor each batch from fermentation to bottling to ensure the best wine possible. Because of this, they have the confidence to offer a 100% satisfaction guaranteed policy. The reason they can do this, is because they've had a lot of trial and error in their past winemaking endeavors.

"It was a hobby," Ken said. "Something we used to play around with. We started experimenting with kits."

"One morning, back in the mid-nineties," said Vickie, "we awoke to find that the wine we had bottled the previous afternoon before had all popped

their corks during the night. To make matters worse, they were all lying side by side on our kitchen counter. It was a huge mess to say the least!"

"The wine hadn't finished fermenting," Ken explained, "and decided to surprise us—and it did. Happily, we haven't has such a surprise since." Visitors who visit the winery, however, will experience several surprises. "This was the first house in Rising Sun with indoor running water," said Ken. "A windmill in the back pumped water into holding tanks up in the attic and the water was gravity fed into the house."

The house the Fiekerts are referring to is both their home and the winery. Built in 1911, the structure has many touches original to the building. High ceilings, dark wood paneling, and winding staircases are seen throughout. It is suggested guests call first, just to ensure the Fiekerts have not run an errand and will be there to welcome them. Once inside, the Fiekerts lead visitors into their wine cellar tasting room. There are many amenities to make guests feel welcome and invite them to linger a while. The Fiekerts wanted to promote a fun and casual atmosphere and a billiard table sits in the center of part of the room. Another thing that stands out are the walls filled with writing. Guests are encouraged to leave notes and their signature, as they're a part of the winery; part of what helps to make it successful. Because of this, guests often leave glowing reviews:

"I loved the wine. The people are down to earth and interesting. Overall wonderful experience. Thank you for making our 18th anniversary memorable."
–Serena Stoneburner

"Great people that make great wine!!!!"
–Raye J. Turner

"Thank you for creating such wonderful Christmas gifts for my family and friends this year. Keep Fiekerts Homestead Wines in mind for any personalized gifts you need this year. Yummy and fun!"
–Sarah Turner
with DeVille's Rising Sun Pharmacy

The last review is referring to a unique offering from Fiekerts. They will personalize wine labels for gift giving. People can use their own photos, family crests, or any un-copyrighted image to make wine labels, and then add any text wanted. These are especially popular for weddings, birthdays, and Christmas, but are great ideas for corporate parties or as a marketing tool. The Fiekerts do this a lot for the many organizations in the community they've become involved with including the Red Wolf Sanctuary and Pink Ribbon Girls.

The Fiekerts themselves have been married almost 35 years and have three children. Their generous heart and spirit is felt by anyone who comes into contact with them. Visit Fiekerts Homestead Wines, let them take you through their wine journey, and write your name on the wall so you can become part of their winery. Cheers!

Wines

Pinot Noir
Semi-dry and medium bodied, this wine pairs best with duck and game, but also goes well with cheesy casseroles and beef stews.

Green Apple
Crisp and tart, this wine is like biting into a Granny Smith Apple. It goes well with almost any cheese and adds interest when added to apple cakes and pies.

Pomegranate
A personal favorite, the sweet and tart balance each other in a smooth, easy sipping wine. Pull this one out for movie night snacks, popcorn, corn chips, etc.

Riesling Ice-Style Wine
Ice wine is made by letting ripe grapes stay on the vine until the first hard freeze. The resulting sweet, dessert wine is a delight as an aperitif.

Recipe

Easy Chicken Pasta

Whenever I make this, every family member, from the youngest to the oldest, loves it.

1 cup of Fiekerts Pinot Grigio
4 boneless chicken breasts
1 can cream of chicken soup
1 14.5 oz. can Italian tomatoes
1 14.5 oz. can artichokes, drained
1 package dry Italian dressing
1 8 oz. package cream cheese
1 16 oz. package bow tie pasta
Mozzarella and parmesan cheese, for garnish

Directions:

In a crock pot layer chicken, dry Italian dressing, wine, tomatoes, artichokes, soup, and place cream cheese on top. Cook on low 8 hours. Fix bow tie pasta according to package directions. Drain and stir into crock pot. Serve in bowls and sprinkle with cheeses.

POWERS' WINERY
DILLSBORO

"Get your wine on at Powers' Winery!"
– The Powers' Family

In the picturesque hills of Dillsboro, Indiana in the southeast corner of the state, sits a small home farm winery that welcomes many visitors a year. The Powers—Connie and Pat—along with their six children, have made a business out of the farm they moved to over twenty years ago. Connie and Pat still hold down full-time jobs and love to greet guests on the weekends. Winemaking and owning a winery were never part of their plan, but sometimes plans find you.

"I have a brother," said Pat, "who thought it would be fun to get juice and try his hand at making wine; it didn't turn out well." The idea intrigued Pat's daughter Christy, however, and she bought a home wine making kit. Wine making is often a trial and error effort as so many factors, juice or grapes, temperature, sunlight, etc. can affect the outcome. She kept at it until making wines that garnered a lot of praise from family and friends. Christy and the other Powers were satisfied with this and probably would not have taken it further, except for a serendipitous event.

As a gift, Christy planned a surprise for her cousin's wedding. She made wine and designed custom labels just for their special day. When several people at the wedding asked her to sell them wine, the idea of a winery was first entertained.

All family members are involved in some capacity at the farm and loyal friends have joined them to help with the winery. Kimberli Bell is the vintner/chef. "I like to experiment with different flavors and blends. I like to think about different foods they can be served with and develop wines to enhance them. White Cranberry is the best seller in the sweet wines and it goes great with pork dishes." Some of her other popular creations are Pomegranate, Black Cherry and Fershizzle. Pomegranate is made in memory of Pat's mother, Barbara Powers.

Another person who is a big part of the winery is Jennifer Powers. Jennifer is the event coordinator. She plans, sets up, and serves at their monthly events, including a February Valentine party which has become especially popular. She and Kimberli work together to ensure that every monthly event is a taste sensation. They also give advice to those who may end up with a wine they didn't choose themselves. "If you get a bottle of wine you don't like," explained Kimberli, "add it to a roast or soup. It breaks down the meat where it becomes so tender and adds a depth of flavor to the soup or sauce."

The warm and cozy tasting room encourages friendships to develop and the Powers and their friends work hard to be a part of the process. They want to help people interested in the process of wine and all the nuances of creating good wine by carrying equipment for wine making. This comes from the camaraderie that winemakers from winery to winery have already developed. "If we have something go wrong," said Kimberli, "We can always call Purdue University. They work closely with all of the Indiana wineries and they'll tell us how to fix it."

One of the things they needed advice with early on was how to keep the deer and other animals out of the vineyards so they would have some grapes to make wine. "A red flashing light, about waist high, makes animals think there may be a predator close by." This worked well, but rain and dew worked havoc on the batteries in the lights. "Putting the lights in clear plastic bags make the batteries last a few months." This is long enough to keep the animals away through the harvest season so that the vines do not become a deer all-you-can-eat buffet.

When visiting Powers' Winery, guests will be greeted by a myriad of family pets including cats, dogs, and even chickens, gracious hosts, and wonderful wines. Come and "Get your wine on at Powers' Winery" soon.

Note: Photographs for Powers' Winery were provided by Kathy Woodhouse.

Powers' Winery
10651 IN-262
Dillsboro, IN 47018
812-432-3620

Events: Yes, small events.
  Contact Jennifer Powers

Wines

❧ Millie (Merlot)

This oaked, dry red has a big bold flavor of dark cherries and currant. It pairs well with smoked meats and roasted vegetables.

❧ Libby (Liebfraumilch)

This German-style dry white wine is best served very chilled after dinner with crisp fruit such as pears and apples, and pungent cheeses such as Roquefort.

❧ Dragon Juice (Raspberry Dragonfruit Shiraz)

This exotic sweet wine mixes raspberry and Shiraz in a pleasing blend that enhances spritzers, appetizers, and summer vegetable salads.

❧ Senorita Sangria

This sweet raspberry with extra special pizazz is a customer favorite. Serve in a tall glass filled with ice and frozen strawberries, blueberries, and peach slices.

From the Winery

Braised Short Ribs

1 bottle of Power's Winery Coastal Blend
2 cups unsalted chicken broth
1 small can of tomato paste
2 Tbl. Butter
2 Tbl. Olive oil
2 Tbl. flour
1 small onion, chopped
1 stalk celery, chopped fine
1 large parsnip, chopped fine
½ tsp. horseradish
2 pounds short ribs
Salt and pepper
Buttered egg noodles with parsley for serving

Directions:

In a large Dutch oven or heavy pot, melt butter and add the onion, celery, and parsnip. Cover and cook over medium-high heat until slightly softened; about five minutes. Uncover and cook until the vegetables are lightly browned. Stir in the tomato paste and horseradish. Add flour and stir for one minute. Add wine and chicken broth; bring to a simmer. On slightly higher than medium-high, heat the oil in a large skillet, season the ribs with salt and pepper and add them to the skillet. Turn until browned well, about 15 minutes. Move the short ribs into the sauce on the Dutch oven. Partially cover, and cook on medium-low heat until very tender; around two hours.

Boil water for noodles. While waiting, remove bones from ribs. While heat is still low, take a large tablespoon, set it on any pocket of oil and tip it slightly into pockets to skim off any oil. Don't worry about removing it all. It's okay to lose a little of the sauce too. Turn heat to med-high to boil. Reduce and thicken sauce to about two cups. Cook noodles according to package directions and put on serving plate. Pour sauce and ribs over noodles. Serve.

HOLTKAMP WINERY
NEW ALSACE

"In vino veritas (In wine truth)"
– Alcaeus

Doug Holtkamp started the path to winery involvement around 2000. He mentioned how much he liked the big, dry red wines and how he'd like to learn how to make them. His wife, Julie was listening. "She bought me a home winemaking kit as a gift and I jumped right in. A friend deemed my first batch, 'not quite drinkable.'" For some, this is the end of their winemaking pursuits, for others, it spurs them to find why it didn't turn out as they hoped and they keep trying to find perfection in order to share it with others. Doug fell into the latter category.

He's learned quite a bit since then. To get what he feels are the best dry reds, he brings grapes from California and Oregon. "Barrel aged dry reds are our specialty," Doug said. Although he's most fond of the dry reds, Doug doesn't shy away from trying other types of wines in order to please every palate that walks through the door of the winery or tasting room. His watermelon won double gold at the Indy International Wine Competition and was runner up for the fruit wine of the year. Robert Reserve, Holtkamp's signature dry red, is named after Doug's father and Sweet Marie is Doug's grandmother, who is 100. "If you want more time," quipped Doug, "drink more wine." Holtkamp opened to the public in 2013 and expanded to open a tasting room in 2016.

212

Although well on his way to a successful boutique winery now, it took a bit of trial and error to get there. "I planted 90 Vidal vines. I thought I killed them all but Jeff found two in the patch of weeds that took over." Jeff is Jeff McCann, an expert on grapes and wine who first planted grapes at the age of 13 for his summer job. After that, he became intrigued with all of the factors involved with planting the vines to making award winning wine. A good wine is one you like. Jeff is the vineyard manager and co-winemaker at Holtkamp. They started with three acres of grapes and expanded in 2015 to add some types often seen in Indiana, Cayuga and Traminette, for example, and some not so well known, such as Dornfelder and Petite Amie. "To take my passion and Jeff's experience," Doug explained, "I metaphorically jumped to the front of the line in creating a winery." Along with the fantastic views and wines, history buffs will find another reason to visit Holtkamp Winery.

"The house was built in 1860," said Doug. "General John Hunt Morgan made a trail through here that the Confederate army followed. In the cellar, there are hooks to lower wine barrels." That people built homes in that era with special features specifically for wine, shows the importance of the wine industry in America at the time of the Civil War. The stones for the foundation were quarried from the farm. Unfortunately, tours are not available. The lovely landscaping sets off both the Holtkamp Winery and home. Doug's parents owned a landscape business that he worked for, and the experience shows in the beautiful layout of the trees and plantings. The pond has a fountain and when visitors sit on the back deck, the vineyard stretches out beyond the pond. Sharing a bottle in these picturesque surroundings, people could easily imagine they are sitting in the French countryside. Santé!

Holtkamp Winery
10868 Woliung Road
New Alsace, IN 47041
513-602-5580

Tasting Room:
6781 Harrison Avenue
Cincinnati, OH 45247

Events: Yes, up to 150, call for details

Wine Trail: Indiana Win

Wines

Robert Reserve

This award winning signature dry wine blend, is barrel aged for fourteen months. Pair with elegant crown roast, or your favorite grilled beef or venison.

Avery White

Indiana grown semi-dry white blended wine. It's fruity and floral with pineapple and grapefruit characteristics. Pair it with a pecan crusted grouper, lightly fried, with Hollandaise sauce.

Sweet Marie

This sweet rosé wine blend is fruity and complex. A blush wine will complement almost any meal. Sip next to a campfire with s'mores.

Watermelon

A sweet, delicious taste of summer in a glass, this wine is a go to for any party, picnic, sangria, or girls' weekend trip.

Recipe

Crispy Chicken

¾ cup Holtkamp Winery's Avery
   White Wine
¼ cup orange juice
One whole chicken cut into eight
   pieces
1 Tbl. Seasoned salt
1 tsp. fresh ground pepper
½ tsp. onion salt
1 tsp. garlic powder
1 tsp. paprika

Directions:

Preheat broiler. Place all seasonings in a plastic bag and shake. Place chicken over rack on a broiler pan or other shallow pan. Spray rack with oil. Sprinkle seasoning mix on both sides of chicken. Place chicken, skin side up, on rack and broil to brown top and set seasonings. Turn oven down to 350°. Mix together wine and orange juice and pour about 1/4 cup into pan, but not over chicken. Bake 15 minutes and baste carefully, so as not to wash off seasonings. Keep cooking, basting with additional wine and orange juice mixture every 15 minutes. About one hour after broiling, check for doneness by cutting into the thickest part of the chicken to check that the juices are running clear, not red or pink. Remove chicken to platter and put pan with wine and juice back into oven for a few minutes to thicken for gravy. Serve with chicken.

AT THE BARN WINERY
LAWRENCEBURG

"Carpe Vinum (seize the wine)"
– The Stutz Family

Although At the Barn Winery is one of the newest in the state of Indiana, it's been a forty year journey for Don and Debby Stutz. Don started experimenting with wine making about the time he and Debby married. Their first baby was quite a big surprise, because it turned out to be triplets. The next baby came along eighteen months later. "Now you know why we drink," joked Debby. After the children came along, Don stopped making wine for a number of years, but picked up the hobby again about ten years ago. That was the first inkling that a winery might be a possibility. Still, the Stutzs took their time to ensure everything was done right.

In about 2003, Don started to restore his great-grandfather's barn on the property. Although repairs were necessary over the years to the barn built in the 1870s, a full restoration had never been undertaken. The wood beams and timbers were power washed to the honeyed look they now have. The reason for restoring the barn was twofold; the family had grown too large and they needed a place they could all gather and the Stutzs wanted a small farm winery as a retire-

ment hobby. "You can't walk outside and spit without hitting some of Donny's family's property," said Debby. "It was definitely a challenge," said Don. "But important to the family that the barn be restored." They consider it a blessing to have a venue where their large family can come together for special occasions.

After the barn, the next thing that needed to be taken care of was the vineyard. The first vines were planted in 2007 and they add different varieties each year for Don's creations. At the Barn currently has Concord, Chancellor, Muscadine, Cayuga White,

216

Niagara, Catawba, and Traminette grape vines, along with berries, apple and peach trees, and a lone pear tree. Don has officially retired and become vintner and winemaker. He makes everything in small batches, twenty-five gallons, and it's very labor intensive; Don works about 60 hours a week at his retirement hobby. While an amateur winemaker, Don entered a lot of contests across the country and won many awards. The winery opened in 2014 and their first competition as a commercial winery was in 2015. One of the wines that won a medal came about because of a very sweet lady; Don's mother Thelma.

"Mom's in her 90s," said Don. "We asked her to try one of the wines, a sweet red. She kept making suggestions and we kept changing it until she felt it was just right. Thelma's Sweet Red was the result and the judges were impressed. Other wines at the winery have garnered much praise, and a little aggravation from Don and Debby's children. Don tends to make wines based on his and Debby's whims or suggestions from customers. Many times, their two sons and two daughters would come to like a wine, and Don wouldn't make it again. Finally, Don made a very popular concoction called BBR (Blueberry, Blackberry, and Raspberry.) The Stutz children all said this was the wine he had to keep making and should always keep on hand. Don obliged, but also does a lot of experimentation with whatever fruits and/or juices he can find. Despite all of his passion and hard work, Don has a quirky side too.

"We want to keep it small because it's a retirement hobby," he laughed while glancing around the packed room, "but we're having trouble keeping it small." We saw this firsthand as the entire winery was full from when we arrived until after we'd left. Despite this, Debby and Don made us feel welcomed and took the time to speak with us and let us try their wonderful wines. Stop by At the Barn Winery soon and see if you can help the Stutzs keep it small.

At the Barn Winery
4152 North Dearborn Road
Lawrenceburg, IN 47025
513-519-8745

Events: Yes, indoors, up to 30

Wines

Chancellor

This wine, made from a hybrid grape, is red and fruit forward flavors of dark berries are the most notable. Pairs well with hamburgers or grilled lamb.

Muscadine

This grape, native to many Southern states, produces a smooth and sweet red wine. Pour half and half in a glass with lemon-lime soda, and squeeze in lime for an extra zing.

Niagara

This wine, bursting with pure grape flavor, is also a table grape. It's versatile and pairs with spicy cuisines, savory appetizers, and nutty quinoa dishes.

Black Raspberry

A family favorite, this sweet and tart wine blend pairs well with sharp cheddar cheese, add to a cobbler, or cook to thicken, allow to cool, and pour over ice cream.

From the Winery

Shrimp Tacos

Pair this delicious Mexican treat with At the Barn Viognier.

1 ½ lbs. uncooked shrimp
4 Tbls. olive oil
1 tsp. garlic salt
1 Tbls. chili powder
2 limes
1 cup mayonnaise
2 Tbls. cilantro
1 Tbls. honey
2 chipotle peppers
Salt
Tortillas
Pico de Gallo
Shredded purple cabbage

Directions:

Marinate shrimp in olive oil, garlic salt, chili powder, and juice of one lime for 15 minutes. Stir often. Meanwhile, make Chipotle sauce. Mix mayonnaise, cilantro, honey, Chipotles, juice from one lime and a pinch of salt. Mix well in food processor.

Cook shrimp in skillet brushed with olive oil until pink (about three minutes).

Build tacos using warmed tortillas, Pico de Gallo, shrimp, purple cabbage (shredded), fresh cilantro and Chipotle sauce on top.

CHATEAU POMIJE WINERY
GUILFORD

"Great memories begin at Chateau Pomije!"
– The Anevski Family

The view while driving up to Chateau Pomije winery is breathtaking. Vineyards stretch on both sides of the road and guide visitors to an impressive stone building with arched porticos and paved walkways. From the back of the building, a beautiful patio overlooks a gazebo and lake. Outdoors or inside, the picturesque setting can be enjoyed while sipping wine and savoring a meal offered by the winery.

Chateau Pomije's Vineyard Café, located inside the winery, is filled with rustic charm. A two story stone fireplace sits on one wall, while the wagon wheel light fixtures draw your attention upwards. A shiny wood floor gives the whole room a warm glow as visitors enjoy their meals. They describe it as "fine dining in a casual atmosphere." The menu offerings are sure to fit anyone's palate with appetizers such as artisanal cheese plates and bruschetta, and entrees such as blackened tilapia and even baby back ribs. This little slice of heaven in Southern Indiana, began as a dream for a determined couple.

Dr. and Mrs. Donald Schumirck wanted to build a winery that would rival the wineries of Europe; the unusual name of the winery is Mrs. Schumirck's maiden name. Many Indiana people were making wines and winning national and international awards with them, and the Schumricks believed there was no reason why they should not try also. They planted the original vineyards and the family worked them and enjoyed the country lifestyle to-

gether. When they decided to build the winery and restaurant, they looked to the buildings already on the farm for inspiration.

One of the original barns on the property, a large two-story structure, was deconstructed and moved to the current location where it was reconstructed. After the winery, which opened in 1987, built up its clientele, the rooms for the tasting bar, Lakeview Room, kitchen, and Grand Ballroom with adjoining kitchen, were added to fill the needs of the growing winery.

Chateau Pomije became known for their involvement in the community, hosting many charity events and community happenings. While doing this, the reputation grew for their renowned restaurant, and their fine wines. The Schumricks took great pride in the simple country charm and hospitality they offered and trained their family and staff to ensure this was experienced by every visitor. Their pride in the winery can be seen in the care they used to develop it toward the meeting place it has become.

Today, the Anevski Family now hosts visitors to Chateau Pomije Winery, but they have the same vision and passion that the Schumrick Family did. They take great pride in sharing their wines with friends and family. Since most of the wines are estate grown, the Anevskis see the product from ground to customer. In their own words: "Our family invites you to share a glass of wine, break bread with us, and enjoy the country charm of Chateau Pomije. You may have a special occasion in the future, like a wedding, a birthday or anniversary, or you may be hosting a corporate event… Chateau Pomije is the perfect place for your special event."

Yes, it's the perfect place for a special event, or just an ordinary drive in the country for an extraordinary experience. Cheers!

Chateau Pomije Winery
25043 Jacobs Road
Guilford, IN 47022
812-623-8004
1-800-791-WINE

Events: Yes, call for details

Wines

❧ Vranac

A smooth, dry red wine, it's mostly grown and made in the Mediterranean region. It has red berries on the nose and a subtle jammy flavor. Pairs well with beef and vegetable dishes like goulash, beef stew, and shepherd's pie.

❧ Sunset Crush

This award winning wine tastes as if you are biting into a juicy green apple. Pair with a dish of cheese and spicy meats.

❧ Domain Reserve

A semi-dry white French hybrid wine that we barrel ferment to make this wine comparable to Chardonnay. This rich wine complements seafood and white meat.

❧ Nectar Kiss

This sweet and fruity wine bursts with the flavor of peach. In saucepan, add small can of peaches and juice, add ½ cup Nectar Kiss, boil to thicken. Pour over pie, cake, or ice cream.

From the Winery

Seafood Linguine

1 ½ cups Chateau Pomije Chardonnay
1 pound fresh shrimp, peeled and deveined
½ pound mussels in shells, steamed
1 pound of linguine
1 small can of peas, drained
2 cloves of garlic, minced
4 Tbls. of favorite hot sauce
Juice from one lemon
3 Tbls. butter
3 Tbls. olive oil
Chopped fresh parsley for garnish
Salt and pepper to taste

Directions:

Cook linguine according to package directions. Put olive oil in a large skillet over medium-high heat. Add the garlic and cook for two minutes. Add 2 tablespoons of butter to the pan, melt and add the shrimp. Cook for one minute. Add wine and bring to a boil, reduce heat, add hot sauce. Simmer about five minutes, until the liquid reduces. Add the remaining butter, lemon juice, and peas. Heat through. Drain linguine and add to skillet. Salt and pepper to taste. Add steamed mussels. Place all in large serving dish and sprinkle with parsley. Serve immediately.

ERTEL CELLARS WINERY
BATESVILLE

"When starting a business, you have to love it. It has to be a part of you to be a success."
– Tom Ertel

Supposedly, nothing is perfect. However, for visitors and staff at Ertel Cellars Winery, perfection is a word that often crosses their lips. "I haven't had to hire new staff for years," said dining room manager Karen Staples. "I've served people who have driven from three hours away to eat dinner. Then the next weekend, they're here again."

Ertel Cellars Winery is a family pursuit, but guests are likely to find owner Tom Ertel mingling in the dining room or guiding cellar tours; which we highly recommend. "You have to build an excellent quality product and people will follow," Tom explained. The building that houses the restaurant and winery is only one example of the quality products at Ertel Cellars.

The cavernous room's beautiful white oaked panel ceiling is noticeable as soon as one walks into the winery. "I hired an architect and started with the idea of a 6/12 pitched roof because that's what many barn ceilings are," said Tom. "Everything else evolved from that idea." The materials and work for the winery are all local, with one exception; the slate floor entryway

came from a quarry in the Dominican Republic. When Ertel saw it, it just had the feel of a winery. The idea of having a winery itself evolved slowly.

In 1990, Ertel bought a piece of land catty-corner to the farm. Farms in this area of Batesville had not gone up for sale in one hundred years or more, as they're often passed down to family members. Ertel bought another piece of ground along the highway. Then, the owner of the farm approached him to buy it. A CPA by trade, Ertel looked for something that

224

Ertel Cellars Winery
3794 East County Road 1100
  North
Batesville, IN 47006
812-933-1500

Events: Yes, indoors up to 130;
  outdoors up to 50

Trail: Southeastern Indiana
  Wine Trail

would be profitable for the land. They started planting grapes to sell to other wineries. Tom's brother Gary Ertel is in charge of maintenance for the vineyard; a job he does well. His sister Patti is responsible for all of the business office activities. They hired Brian Ahaus as winemaker and he is just as particular about ensuring everything is perfect where the wine is concerned. The Cabernet Sauvignon is a three year process from the time the grapes are picked.

With everything Ertel Cellars has to offer, visitors from nearby and far away may be found at the winery at any time. Plan to eat at the restaurant whenever you come for a visit, but be sure to make reservations. Although the Ertels do not advertise, the dining room is usually packed. Cheers!

Wines

Chambourcin

Full-bodied dry red wine with hints of cherry and date flavors. It pairs well with red meat and wild game.

Vignoles

A light and crisp white wine with a hint of sweetness and tropical flavors. Pairs well with savory or spicy foods.

Blush Table Wine

This crisp blush wine is Ertel Cellar's version of White Zinfandel. It will pair up with any appetizer or entrée.

Pink Catawba

A very fruity wine, smooth and easy to drink, it goes well with chicken and seafood salad, as well as appetizers and picnic foods.

From the Winery

Filet with Bordelaise Sauce and Asparagus with Hollandaise

Set an 8 oz. beef filet on the counter thirty minutes before cooking.

Bordelaise Sauce
2 cups Ertel Cellars Cabernet Sauvignon
2 cups beef stock
2 shallots, chopped
2 cloves garlic, chopped
3 Tbl. butter

In small saucepan, caramelize the onions and garlic in the butter. Add the wine and reduce by half. Add the beef stock and reduce by half again. Strain through a cheese cloth and keep warm.

Salt and pepper both sides of the filet, then dab with paper towels to dry. Sear in sauté pan on high heat, six minutes on each side. Turn off heat and let steak sit for five minutes.

Hollandaise Sauce
6 egg yolks

1 oz. Ertel Cellars Chardonnay
1 tsp. kosher salt
1 Tbl. lemon juice
1 tsp cayenne pepper
2 sticks butter melted

Place egg yolks in a metal bowl and set over a double boiler set at low-medium. If the sauce gets too hot, it will separate. Whisking the entire time, add the wine, salt, lemon juice, and pepper. One ounce or less at a time, add the butter and incorporate with the whisk. Sauce will become thick, rich, and creamy. Keep warm on very low heat.

Trim bottom ends off of a small bundle of asparagus. Drop into boiling water and leave in until water boils again. Pull out and put in ice bath. Pat dry and wrap prosciutto around the bundle. Roast in a 350° oven for eight minutes.

Arrange the plate with mashed potatoes and steak served with the bordelaise sauce and asparagus with hollandaise.

The Southern Region

FRENCH LICK WINERY & THE VINTAGE CAFE • *West Baden Springs, Orange County*

PATOKA LAKE WINERY • *Birdseye, Dubois County*

QUIBBLE HILL WINERY • *Depauw, Harrison County*

HUBER'S ORCHARD WINERY & VINEYARDS • *Borden, Clark County*

INDIAN CREEK WINERY • *Georgetown, Floyd County*

RIVER CITY WINERY • *New Albany, Floyd County*

BEST VINEYARDS WINERY • *Elizabeth, Harrison County*

TURTLE RUN WINERY • *Corydon, Harrison County*

SCOUT MOUNTAIN WINERY AND BED & BREAKFAST • *Corydon, Harrison County*

WINZERWALD WINERY • *Bristow, Perry County*

MONKEY HOLLOW WINERY • *Ferdinand, Dubois County*

MYSTIQUE WINERY • *Lynnville, Warrick County*

HEDGEGROVE MEADERY AND WINERY • *Cynthiana, Posey County*

LITTLE CREEK WINERY • *Evansville, Vanderburgh County*

PEPPER'S RIDGE WINERY • *Rockport, Spencer County*

BLUE HERON VINEYARDS AND WINERY • *Cannelton, Perry County*

Additional Wineries
(see page 294 for information)

CHATEAU DE PIQUE TASTING ROOM • *812-725-7879*

MONKEY HOLLOW WINERY AND BISTRO AT THE HISTORIC
    WOLLENMANN HOME • *812-998-2112*

WINZERWALD WINERY EVANSVILLE TASTING ROOM • *812-423-2427*

FRENCH LICK WINERY & THE VINTAGE CAFE
WEST BADEN SPRINGS

"What started as a hobby has now become a legacy."
– The Dotys

Seeing the majestic mansions, elegant hotels, and clear waterways while driving to this winery, one may feel as if they're in the Loire Valley of France or the Tuscany region of Italy. Almost next door to French Lick Winery sits West Baden Springs Hotel. Built over a century ago, this luxury spa and resort offers much for visitors. People stroll through expansive gardens, take carriage or trolley rides around the property relax on massive balconies and verandas, or stare in wonder at what is often referred to as "the eighth wonder of the world;" the central dome. When built, it was the largest dome in the world and one feels incredible small when standing in the atrium area, gazing seven stories up toward the ceiling. A visit here is a definite must when in the area. Also in the area is a place to sit, sip, and reflect on all of the elegance the area has to offer.

Owner John Doty has a long history with wine making and experimentation. From the age of around twelve, he learned to make many things on his grandfather's dairy barn in Dubois, Indiana. Cottage cheese, butter, root beer, and homebrew were some of the things he learned, but he was also introduced to winemaking using the Concord grapes and blackberries that grew on the farm. As a young boy, he would take to heart his grandfather's lessons. "What I remember most was the smell of fermentation," he recalled. "It's quite pungent and a smell I still enjoy." While John Doty pursued his degree in

Farm and Business management at Purdue University, he met Kim Klingle, who would later become Kim Doty. While starting his career in banking, John continued to make wine and share it with friends and family. After he and Kim married in 1978 and moved to Huntingburg, she became just as enthusiastic about the wine industry. Together they explored the burgeoning home farm wine business.

The couple had long dreamed of having their own business and they wanted to preserve a farm that had been in Kim's family for more than 100 years. "Having a legacy to leave to our children and grandchildren was also appealing," added Kim. While still working their full-time jobs, John as a loan officer and Kim as a postal worker, they took the plunge, opening the winery in 1995. They bought the grapes at first, planting their Heaven's View Vineyard in 1998. It was the first winery in Indiana to plant Norton grapes. The vineyard also contains several other popular varieties such as Cabernet Franc, Noiret, Steuben, and Vidal varietals. The vineyards were a family affair from the beginning with their sons Aaron and Nick often helping out with the labor intensive agri-business. Now grown, they are an integral part of the winery.

They first opened in the historic Beechwood Mansion in French Lick but growing pains, the good kind, spurred them to renovate the old Kimball piano factory into the new winery and opera-

French Lick Winery
  & The Vintage Café
8145 West Sinclair Street
West Baden Springs, IN 47469
812-936-2293

Events: No

Trail: Indiana Uplands Wine Trail

tions building, opening in 2005. With the added floor space, the Dotys were able to include something that earns rave reviews from visitors; The Vintage Café. Specializing in Italian fare, the Dotys took extra care to ensure the authenticity of the foods. Their signature pizza dough is made from a starter that began in Naples, Italy over 200 years ago. Generally, a starter is a simple substance of flour, water, and some type of yeast. It's left out to ferment, and then used to make different types of bread. After using some of it, the starter is then re-fed with flour and water and refrigerated before being pulled out to ferment and begin the process again.

This dedication to food is also seen in the wine, which has garnered medals in nearly every local, national, and international competition the Dotys have entered. Their employees at the tasting bar are fully trained and are often asked what is the best wine to drink. Their advice is, "Drink what you like, how you like it, with foods you like." Be sure to visit the French Lick area soon. Plan to stay a few days and soak in the atmosphere of an era that is now hard to find.

Note: Photographs for French Lick Winery were provided by Kathy Woodhouse.

Wines

Heaven's View Vidal

Estate grown white wine with crisp green apple and tropical fruit flavors. Pair it with roasted vegetables with balsamic vinegar or broiled bruschetta with mozzarella and tomato relish.

Leon Millot

Semi-dry red wine overflowing with blackberry and vanilla aromas with cherry flavors. Serve this wine with most meals and appetizers.

Tropical Frost

A very sweet dessert wine with delicate tropical fruit flavors, this wine is a wonderful aperitif or adds zing to a fruit punch.

French Tickle

This sweet bubbly blush with tangy citrus flavors is wonderful for special celebrations or every day.

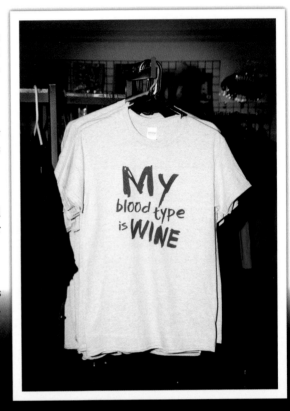

From the Winery

French Lick Winery Wine Cake Recipe

"We've been serving this cake in our restaurant for over ten years and it is still our most popular dessert!"

Cake
1 cup French Lick Red Wine
1 package white cake mix
1 package grape gelatin
⅔ cup vegetable oil
3 eggs

Glaze
¾ cup French Lick Red
1 stick real butter
½ pound confectioner's sugar

Preheat oven to 350°. Coat a Bundt pan with non-stick cooking spray, coat with flour and set aside. In large bowl, combine cake mix and gelatin; add oil and one cup of wine. Mix until just combined. Add eggs one at a time, mixing well after each. Pour into prepared pan and bake for fifty minutes or until cake tests done.

While cake is baking, mix butter, sugar, and ¾ cup of wine in a small saucepan. Simmer over low heat while cake bakes; butter should be completely melted. Pour glaze over cake as soon as it comes out of the oven; cake will sizzle. Let stand for 20 minutes before turning onto a wire rack. Let cool completely. Sprinkle with confectioner's sugar. Serves 12-16.

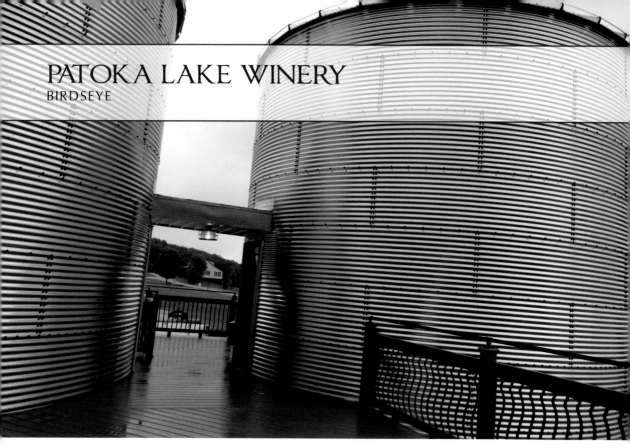

PATOKA LAKE WINERY
BIRDSEYE

"Uncork the possibilities"

Patoka Lake is the second largest reservoir in the state of Indiana at almost 9,000 acres. As lake-goers drive up to the entrance on North Dillard Road in Birdseye, they will pass one of the newest wineries of Indiana, Patoka Lake Winery. Although a recent edition to Indiana wineries, the five owners have been involved in wine and/or winemaking for a number of years.

"We've been doing the wine cruises for about five years," said part-owner Heather Setser. "We tossed around the idea of opening a winery and we decided to do it." These sunset cruises on Patoka Lake are very popular and sell out often. They do sunset cruises the second and fourth Fridays of the month during June, July, and August. Fall foliage cruises are every Saturday in September and October. While on Patoka Lake, you may see a phenomenon many people are unaware of.

They have what's known as a freshwater jellyfish, but there's no need to worry; they don't sting. The small, translucent creatures are hard to see, as they're about the size of a penny. Although prolific in much of the United States, they aren't often noticed. Not originally native to the United States, the freshwater jellyfish were thought to have been carried here in aquatic plants from China. They are just one of the unique features of this area of Southern Indiana.

Patoka Lake Winery
2900 North Dillard Road
Birdseye, IN 47513
812-685-2203, ext. 3

Events: Yes, up to 250
    indoors or out

Question: When was the Corkscrew designed?
Answer: The first patent for a corkscrew was
applied for in England in the late 1700s.

Open as of June 3, 2016, Patoka Lake Winery is unique because of two suites that are located in new silos built for holding guests instead of grain. These cozy suites include a kitchenette, living room, and fireplace. Upstairs you'll find a skillfully built wooden plank ceiling above a king-sized bed. Along with these rooms, Patoka Lake Winery has many lovely guest houses and cabins available for rent.

Inside the winery, the Barrel Room, an unusual wood paneled round room, is available for parties. It's set off by paddock doors, giving the winery a ranch-style feel. "The inspiration for the building was 'It's Southern Indiana,' said Setser. "It's farmland, it's farms, it's agriculture and we wanted to do something unique and different." The tasting room is light and airy with post beams and honeyed wood walls. There's a large dairy case filled with selections of cheeses and meats to pair with your favorite glass of wine. It's a space that invites visitors to linger and find new friends in a relaxed atmosphere.

The winery has opened with nice selections of wines with plans to have many more. The focus is on a craft winery with a lot of different blends. "My grandfather made everything into alcohol and introduced that to me," said part-owner Steve Bartels. "I continued the tradition at college, with beer and wine at the fraternity. When I built a house, I actually added a room onto the garage for beer and wine making." He created a wine in the German tradition called Das Afpel Riesling, a perfected combination of apple and Riesling wine. They also offer a Classic Series of fruit wines with a Blackberry, Blueberry, and Catawba, and an Artisan Blend Series with selections such as a cherry-apple-blueberry blend called Red, White, and Blue. Whatever your wine choice, you can't find a better way to spend a day, or two, than bringing friends and sipping crisp wine on a porch with beautiful views and enjoying the wonderful hospitality of the folks from Patoka Lake Winery. Cheers!

Wines

✣ Merlot

This dry red wine is smooth and structured with fruity and earthy flavors. It pairs well with red meats and side dishes such as a mushroom filled baked potato.

✣ Riesling

The floral aromas and luscious flavors of apple, pear, and peach highlight the crispness of this white wine. Pair with salami wrapped mozzarella or jam slathered brie cheese.

✣ Cherry

Sweet and fruity, this wine is as sweet and flavorful as a pie. Take it on a camping trip and pair it with s'mores, brownies, or other favorite chocolate desserts.

✣ Blackberry

Like picking them straight off the bush, this wine is summer in a glass. In a saucepan, cook one cup wine with 1/2 tsp each of cinnamon and nutmeg until boiling. Cool, whisk in 1/2 cup powdered sugar and spread over a spice or jam cake.

Pairing

We like to pair Patoka Lake Winery's Riesling with cream soups. We suggest the Oh-La-Lobster Bisque on page 52, (Country Heritage) but any meatless cream-based soup, or one with chicken or seafood, would pair well.

QUIBBLE HILL WINERY
DEPAUW

"It's our commitment to produce fine quality, handcrafted wines with attention to detail."
– Jamie and Steve Kraft

The owners of Quibble Hill Winery, Jamie and Steve Kraft, thought long and hard before coming up with a name. "A Quibble is a minor objection," revealed Jamie. "To whine is to snivel and complain. So come out to wine a bit!"

There's little to quibble about here, but definitely try the wine. The two-story log cabin is a welcoming place. Rockers beckon visitors to come and stay awhile. The beautiful view is relaxing and strangers become friends on the covered porch. The Krafts have owned the property for over twenty years, but the sight never ceases to amaze them as they often sip a glass of wine together while watching the sun set. When they bought the land, they never imagined that it would become a business one day, but they'd always wanted to work for themselves.

"Before he died," Jamie explained, "Dad said 'Do something you want to do. Don't work for someone else until you're 65 and then retire.'" Jamie and Steve both worked full-time jobs; she in advertising, he as head of maintenance at a chemical company. As a respite from their busy lifestyle, they began visiting wineries in Southern Indiana and Northern Kentucky. They bought some small wine kits to try their hand at making their own wine, and some didn't turn out too bad. All the while, the thought of owning their own business was a topic of discussion.

"Let's build a winery," Steve said one day out of the blue.

Quibble Hill Winery
338 Gowers Lane NW
Depauw, IN 47115
502-424-9559

Events: No

Jamie looked at him with a ready answer. "Are you crazy?"

After agonizing for a few years, they decided it was something they wanted to try. They began clearing a corner of the property that used to be a duck pond and contained mostly scrub trees. At the same time, they were volunteering at another local winery helping to make wine and learn the craft. "We knew we wanted to start with sweet wine," Steve advised. This is because 80% of Indiana wine drinkers want sweet wine. Although Quibble Hill Winery opened in February of 2014, they now have five dry, a semi-sweet, a tart Diamond wine, five sweet, and two sangria varieties; something for everyone. "We're trying to get unique wines that you don't find just anywhere," said Steve. "So far," Jamie added, "we have no blends; it's all straight fruit."

The Krafts took pride in designing and building their winery. With the two-story log cabin structure, the bottom floor is the fermentation and production area, while the top floor is the winery. Steve built the unique bar, putting drawer pulls into the concrete top to hang purses and jackets. Visitors will often find regulars sitting around it chatting with the friendly Krafts and drinking their favorite wines. Golden, knotty pine walls continue the outside cabin feel and fun pictures and sayings are conversation pieces.

To further enjoy Quibble Hill's indoor and outdoor spaces, a painting class is held once a month and live music is offered at the pavilion every Saturday from May through September. Guests can enjoy a picnic table or one of the rocking chairs on the porch (or bring their own chairs). They are picnic friendly or you can purchase meat and cheese trays from the tasting room. We can't think of a better way to put a summer Saturday to bed. Cheers!

Wines

❧ Big Thunder

A Malbec wine, this dry red offers nuanced flavors of blackberry and plum. It pairs well with sirloin and flank steaks, dark poultry; and a must try with white chocolate.

❧ Mornin' Mist

This semi-sweet white wine, made from the Muscat grape, is music on the tongue. This wine adds interest to pair with lemon desserts, or add to sauces for shellfish.

❧ Porch Punch

A sweet Niagara wine, with smooth grape flavor, this will be a favorite porch sipping wine, or serve at a dessert party.

❧ Lacy's Ledge

Sweet concord at its finest. Serve with a plate of your favorite chocolate cookies.

From the Winery

Sautéed Mushrooms with Stonewall Jaxun Reduction

½ cup Quibble Hill Stonewall Jaxun wine
2 Tbsp. butter
2 cloves of garlic
2 8 oz Packages of sliced mushrooms
1 tsp. fresh thyme

Directions:

Sauté mushrooms in butter, garlic, and thyme until tender. Season with salt and pepper. Add wine and reduce.

These are good as a side dish, as a potato topping, or with a nice beef filet.

HUBER'S ORCHARD, WINERY & VINEYARDS
BORDEN

"Quality is homegrown"
– Ted Huber

The motto at Huber's Orchard and Winery is a simple statement, "Quality is homegrown." While sitting on the patio and looking out across their pond to green vineyards stretched as far as the eye can see, the visitor understands that simple statement contains hard work and generations of farming experience.

In 1843, when Simon Huber arrived from Baden-Baden, Germany and purchased 80 acres in Southern Indiana, he brought generations of agricultural training that had been handed down to him, along with the skill of wine making. The seventh generation of his family is still living and working on the now over 600 acre farm. To make the excellent wine at Huber's, Ted Huber explained. "It's all about growing the best possible fruit and using that fruit to produce a great product." The results of their standard of quality can be seen by the array of medals hung along the ceiling won at local, state, national, and international competitions. "We're the only winery in the state to have won a Governor's Cup trophy in each decade since we opened," Huber said. "Twenty-one total. We're also the largest estate winery in Indiana."

Huber's caters to every member of the family and wine is only part of their operation.

"Coming here is an all day, family experience." There are orchards and fields to pick apples, peaches, and strawberries, among other fruits when they're in season. A hay ride takes visitors to a fall pumpkin patch or Christmas tree lot. The farm hosts more than

15,000 school children yearly, introducing them to the process of running a large scale agricultural operation. A cheese shop, a farmer's market, an ice cream factory, and a children's playground area, are among the many

activities offered. But selling products is not what makes Ted Huber excited about his heritage.

"We get to be a part of all aspects of the products we grow," Huber enthused. "We don't just grow and sell to someone. We get to make our products into wine, breads, pies, and many things for people to enjoy." The Starlight Café in the winery offers a variety of sandwiches, salads, and one of the best pizzas I've ever tasted.

Although the family had always made wine for their own use, the idea of opening a winery didn't happen until 1971 after Indiana passed the farm winery law. "Dad and Uncle Carl started investigating the feasibility of planting and opening a winery," Huber said. After years of research, classes, travel, and planting grapes, the Hubers applied for their winery license in 1976, had it granted in 1977, and opened the winery in 1978. "I really applaud them for going about it correctly," Huber acknowledged. "There is a huge difference between an amateur wine maker and making wine on a commercial scale." Many wineries fail within the first few years, but Huber's Orchard and Winery is thriving because of the hard work and quality put into it by generations of this family dedicated to their agricultural roots. Come and try some of the wonderful selections in the winery tasting room, a converted barn originally built in 1938, and sip the history of generations of Hubers.

Quibble Hill Winery
19816 Huber Road
Borden, IN 47106
812-923-9813
812-923-9463

Events: Yes, indoor seating up, t
1,500; outdoor seating, several
thousand

Trail: Indiana Uplands Wine Tr

Wines

Huber's has a large selection of wines, distillations, ports and infused wines.

❧ Malbec

This estate-grown dry red wine carries the aromas of fig and dark cherry with a slight spice. Flavors of black pepper, coffee, a dark berries can be found in this complex wine. Pair with pasta, steak or a tart berry dessert.

❧ Starlight Red

This semi-dry wine is great chilled or at room temperature. Light and fruity with interesting plum and berry aromas, this is the wine to serve with pizza or anything from the grill.

❧ Niagara

A bold and intense semi-sweet wine with hints of grape and tropical fruit flavors. This one pairs with soft cheeses like blue and camembert, a fruit dessert, or as a cocktail spritzer.

❧ Sweet Marcella

This concord is the favorite of many visitors. Created by Marcella Huber, this wine was refined until perfect. First released in 1996, it's a staple year after year. Pair with pork chops, grape salad, or cheddar cheese. A great one to share with friends.

❧ Raspberry Infusion

This dessert wine is not-too-sweet and perfect on its own. Pair it with chocolate desserts for an extra zing.

From the Winery

Baked Brie with Cranberries, Almonds, and Honey

1 small wheel of Brie cheese

1 package crescent rolls

2 Tbls. of your favorite, not too sweet, jelly. We like plum or fig.

2 Tbls. fresh honey

1 Tbls. dried cranberries

1 Tbls. sliced toasted almonds

1 egg white

Roll crescent rolls out to a single layer and seal any perforations. Place cheese wheel in the center and spread with jelly. Pull crescent rolls around and over the top, twisting. Brush the top with egg white using pastry brush. Bake at 350° until browned, 20-25 minutes. Remove from oven and let cool slightly. Transfer to serving plate. Drizzle with honey. Sprinkle with cranberries and almonds. Serve with crackers and Huber's Niagara wine.

Bonus Recipe:

When I make my own pizza sauce, everyone wants to know my secret. It's simple. Pour two 15 oz. cans of Italian tomatoes into a large skillet over medium-high heat, add one cup of Huber's Chambourcin wine. Cook and smash the tomatoes until they thicken to the consistency of pizza sauce; this will take about twenty minutes. Spread over crust, add your favorite toppings, and bake at 375° until crust is golden brown. This recipe also works well as a dipping sauce for bread and other appetizers.

INDIAN CREEK WINERY
GEORGETOWN

"A little sip of friendship on the hill"
– Mark and Mary Jane Kendall

Mark Kendall's first winery experiences were like a secret rite of passage. "My grandpa took me to the smokehouse when I was about nine," Kendall explained. "Until then, I wasn't allowed in there. Grandpa opened the floor and led me down into the cellar where the still was. I helped him pick the grapes and take off the stems to make wine." After that, he helped out every harvest season all the way up to college.

"I went to the army, got married, had a career in construction, then I got hit with health problems and looked at death three times," Kendall stated. He was told his chances weren't good and while waiting to begin the next round of chemo, he went with a work crew to Pennsylvania. On the way back home, he saw a Krispy Kreme Doughnut Shop. Though told he should watch his diet, "I decided doctors weren't going to make my life decisions. I ate doughnuts all the way back to Louisville." This spurred him to drink the most out of life that he could, literally.

What started him back on his winery path were his in-laws. They brought over five gallons of grapes and he decided to make wine with them. After that, he kept making and experimenting with grapes. "People started asking to buy it," Kendall said. "So, I decided to investigate the rules to getting a license and open a winery. I first planted 4 ½ acres of grapes, then found out I was a terrible farmer." He decided to buy all of his fruit and juice from local farmers.

He and his wife Mary Jane are known for their spur of the moment road trips. They've went to Mobile, Alabama to eat oysters, Nashville, Tennessee for barbecue, and Virginia Beach, Virginia for a seafood buffet, just to name a few. During all of these travels, they would stop at the wineries along the way, so they had a pretty good idea of what they wanted the winery to look like. With his building experience, Kendall has created a space to welcome all guests. The tasting bar is a large u-shaped stone structure, topped by a unique concrete lid. Tile floors and tall wood ceilings are highlighted by the warm atmosphere of the cozy tasting room, while large windows and double doors let in plenty of natural light.

Many friends and family are involved in the day to day workings of the winery. "We had a combined family and friend tasting party and wine naming contest," explained Kendall. "Some unique names came about that night such as Lilly 'Da' Ville. After a few glasses, you can only say 'Da.'"

Visitors are a welcome sight to the winery dog, Allie. She's very nosy and doesn't want to be left out of anything. She'll patrol from a perch above the tasting room, walking back and forth to make sure she's seen everyone. The Weimaraner earned her name in an unusual fashion. "When she was a pup," Kendall said, "she would chew on people's fingers to tell them she wanted to go out. We called her alligator, which got shortened to Allie." Whether your goal is to try great wines, hear interesting stories, or unwind in a relaxed atmosphere, Indian Creek Winery offers this and so much more.

Note: Photographs for Indian Creek Winery were provided by Kathy Woodhouse.

Indian Creek Winery
6491 County Line Road
Georgetown, IN 47122
502-396-6209

Events: Yes, indoors up to 175

Trail: Hoosier Wine Trail

Question: Which French chemist discovered that wine is created by microscopic organisms also known as yeast?
Answer: In 1857, Louis Pasteur found this and developed a process, now called pasteurization, in which liquids such as wine, beer and milk,are heated to a temperature which kills most of the bacteria and molds that are already present in them.

Wines

⚘ Dry Creek Red

Reminiscent of a blend of Cabernet Sauvignon and Chambourcin, this dry red pairs well with grilled red meats and vegetables. For a special touch, add a cup to your favorite au jus sauce mix or beef gravy and boil to thicken.

⚘ Vidal Blanc

This full-bodied dry contains a buttery feel and slightly floral notes with a crisp pineapple-like finish. This versatile wine pairs with light dishes such as salads and cheese platters, or is excellent with chicken or vegetarian dishes.

⚘ Sweet Creek Rosé

This sweet wine is good to sip alone or pair with s'mores, fruit tarts, or mix into a white sangria with limeade and oranges.

⚘ Blackberry

Sweet and fruity, like eating blackberries straight off the bush. Add a cup to your blackberries for a cobbler, it goes well with a pepperoni pizza or a slice of sharp cheddar cheese.

Recipe

Lily White Teasers

¼ cup Indiana Creek Lily White, plus two tablespoons

2 8 oz. packages of cream cheese, softened

2 Tbls. fresh chopped chives (Chives are not the stem of green onions, but are an herb usually found near lettuces in the grocery store.)

¼ tsp onion salt

4 slices of bacon, cooked crisp, drained and crumbled

2 egg whites

2 cans of crescent rolls

3 Tbls olive oil

1 tsp dried garlic chips

Directions:

In a medium bowl, thoroughly combine wine, cheese, chives, onion salt, and bacon. Unroll crescent rolls and divide at perforations; there should be 16 rolls. Place 1-2 tablespoons on the larger end of each roll, leaving some room at the large end for rolling. Roll up crescent rolls and place on greased cookie sheet. Bake in 325° oven for 20-25 minutes. Serve warm. Mix two tablespoons of wine, garlic chips, and olive oil together for dipping oil.

RIVER CITY WINERY
NEW ALBANY

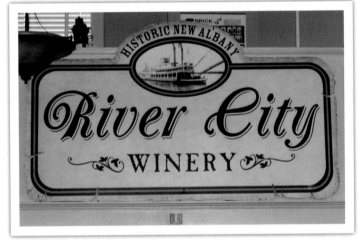

Gary Humphrey had a dream to open a small winery that served pizza, but as often happens, serendipity intervenes and something great happens. "I hired a chef who got bored with making brick oven pizzas and we decided to expand the menu." They're now famous for their crab cakes and crème brûlée and offer a variety of menu items including chicken cordon gouda, pastas, and salmon. This has led to an explosion of expansion at River City and there are plans for more. "We're planning a separate dining room with an art gallery theme, more retail space, and banquet facilities," Humphrey said.

Humphrey was very interested in the revitalization that was happening in the older part of his town of New Albany, Indiana. "When I was a boy, I can only remember one clothing store here. Now there are many residential and business spaces in a several block area." In addition to being happy about the growth happening in the area, Humphrey is very interested in the history of New Albany and preserving its structures.

"This building started in 1898 by a Bavarian clothier named Baer. That business closed in 1932 when he retired. It was taken over by W.T. Grants, a five and

dime." Humphrey took me through the 1937 flood, various other businesses and hard times that led up to the time when he acquired the building. "It had been vacant for three years when I purchased it. There were six inches of water in the basement, which had caused the wood floors to buckle. We removed every board, had them planed, and then re-laid them." Humphrey focused on returning the building to the way it would have looked when first built. "I did all the subcontracting, much of the physical work, and was there every day for the 18 month project."

This may sound exhausting to some, but in addition to that, Humphrey was working a 40 hour week

River City Winery
321 Pearl Street
New Albany, IN 47050
812-945-9463

Tasting Room
25 North Main Street
Franklin, IN 46131
812-945-9463

Events: Yes, indoor only, up to 40

Trail: Hoosier Wine Trail

in law enforcement, as well as figuring out what equipment was necessary for a winery and how to make wine, which he'd never done before. "My very first batch won gold at the Indy International Wine Festival." He knew he was on the right track and pressed on with his business plan, opening to rave reviews in 2009. Humphrey works hard to keep customers happy, offering a variety of events for all including painting nights, music, and special food tastings. There's a small park next to their outdoor patio, which offers free concerts from June to September. In addition, Humphrey is very determined to not lose the historic feel and stories of the entire area.

All of the labels of his wines tell a story of a person, place, or happening in New Albany. For example, after the Civil War ended, Robert E. Lee had a steamboat built in New Albany. "Nicknamed the 'Monarch of the Mississippi'...the steamboat gained its greatest fame for racing and beating the then-current speed record holder, Natchez, in an 1870 steamboat race." (wikipedia.org/wiki/Robert_E._Lee_(steamboat)

With all of the amenities the winery has to offer, excellent service, wine tastings, delicious food, music, and a fun and friendly atmosphere, you may find the hours slipping away as you share fun times at River City Winery.

Wines

❧ Vignoles
Floral notes and a honey-like mouth feel set this wine apart from most Vignoles. Pair with a seared chicken tenderloin or coconut curries.

❧ Market House Cranberry
Just the right hint of sweet with a tart finish, this wine is great chilled for summer drinks or warmed for the winter and fall with a cinnamon swizzle stick.

❧ Black Currant Cyclone
A sweet, earthy taste highlights this fragrant wine. Semi-dry, it pairs with almost any meat.

❧ Catawba
Beautiful blush color accentuates this light and fruity wine. Serve it with barbecue, grilled chops, or Cajun dishes

Recipe

We could not hope to compare to River City Winery's crab cakes, pictured, but here's a recipe we like.

1 pound shredded crabmeat
2 Tbs bread crumbs
1 egg
1 tablespoon creamy ranch dressing
½ tsp yellow mustard
¼ tsp horseradish
2 tsp fresh parsley, chopped
1 tsp smoked paprika
Salt and pepper to taste

Directions:

Set oven to broil. Mix all ingredients except parsley and paprika. Form into patties and place on a lightly greased broiler pan. Broil for 10 to 15 minutes, flipping halfway through, until lightly browned on each side. Sprinkle with parsley and paprika. Pair with River City Winery's Vignoles wine.

BEST VINEYARDS WINERY
ELIZABETH

"We have the 'Best' wines"
– Wilbert Best

In June of 2000, Wilbert Best decided he wanted to buy some land and move into the 1893 farmhouse on the property. The idea of a winery was never intended, but visitors standing on the deck and looking out at the gently rolling hills, will understand why he chose this picturesque spot. Mr. Best's first plan for the farm was to rent to a local farmer as extra crop land for him. "Within six months, that plan fell through when the farmer developed some health problems and had to retire in January of 2001," Best explained.

He and his sisters, Rachel, at first the reluctant participant, and Berretta, who "hopped on the crazy wagon," searched for the perfect crop that didn't take too much time or experience, plus was fun and had a decent return on investment. With some research, they found the area used to be a big grape producing region before Prohibition. By chance, the Indiana Wine Grape Council was holding a meeting close by soon after. They attended and were surprised to find people who could sit around and talk about grapes for eight hours. "It was insane," Best said. "These people were serious about grapes and wine."

At first, the Bests intended to grow table grapes because, "To be honest," Wilbert Best said, "we didn't have a clue about wine, wine grapes, or really anything agricultural." But they were engineers and naturally curious and, well, "curiosity got the cat." They were advised to only grow one acre of grapes in the beginning, about 600 plants, because of the labor intensive routine of a vineyard. However, the Bests found if they ordered 1,000 plants, they'd save 5%. Never one to pass up a bargain, they noticed if they ordered even more, they'd save another 5%. They ended up ordering 2,500 vines and the adventure really began.

At first, they sold grapes to other wineries, but held back a few to experiment. Wine makers with a background heavy in math, such as engineers, tend to make some very good wines and the first batch gave Wilbert an urge to try more varieties until now they have many unique wines including plum, black raspberry, and elderberry.

The winery idea developed over time and in 2008, Best Winery became the 33rd winery to open in Indiana. The cozy gift shop contains pictures of a bygone era, handmade gift items, and often, Shaggy, the neighbor's collie. "He likes to come and visit our dog Blitz," Wilbert laughed. A new addition, a distillery specializing in flavored moonshines, opened in 2016. There is also a plan to have a small commercial kitchen for things like soups and finger food.

Whether your goal is to taste some fine wines or distilled spirits, share some laughs with the owners, sit out under the stars and listen to a summer concert, or visit with the winery dogs, Best Vineyards is the place to be. As Wilbert Best says, "You may have tried some, but come and taste The Best Vineyards' wine."

Note: Photographs for Best Vineyards were provided by Kathy Woodhouse.

Best Vineyards Winery
8373 Morgan's Lane SE
Elizabeth, IN 47117
812-969-9463 (WINE)

Events: Yes, Indoor seating, up to 30; Outdoor seating, up to 250

Trail: Indiana Uplands Wine Trail

Wines

Blitz's Best

An un-oaked blend of Pinot Noir and Zinfandel, pair this flavor delight with roasted chicken or duck, or a favorite beef casserole or stew.

Nouveau

This French Beaujolais-style wine is a blend of Best's Chambourcin, Muscat, and Syrah. Perfect for a Bistro style appetizer party with goose liver paté, a selection of Brie and Camembert cheeses, and a bruschetta with bacon, Italian tomatoes, and cream cheese. Just mix together, spread on thin slices of French bread, and broil a minute or two.

Plum

A personal favorite to sip alone, this delicious sweet and tangy wine goes well with sushi, curried dishes, and plain cheesecake.

Mango

A bestseller, this fruity and refreshing wine has a tropical taste and adds interesting flavor to white sangrias, frozen peach drinks, and even a pot roast.

From the Winery

Chocolate Pâté

¾ cup Hummingbird Red or other red wine
1 pound semi-sweet chocolate, chopped
¼ cup heavy whipping cream

Combine chocolate, wine and cream in top of double boiler and melt over simmering water. Stir constantly until mixture is smooth. Do not allow chocolate to get too warm. Remove from heat and whisk well. Pour into an 8x4" loaf pan lined with wax paper and chill overnight. Remove from refrigerator and allow to warm slightly. Spread on your favorite sugar or vanilla cookies. Easy and delicious!

TURTLE RUN WINERY
CORYDON

"Creating exceptional quality wine that goes with food and friends"
– Jim Pfeiffer

Jim Pfeiffer is used to the question, "How did the winery get its name?"

"The drive sets between two ponds and when I came to look at the property," he explained, "there was a large snapping turtle in the middle of the road. I didn't want to drive over it and it wouldn't move, so I had to find a way to maneuver around it." In honor of that turtle, the winery got a name and a mascot. Tippy the Turtle is a small metal sculpture that regular visitors take with them on trips so they can photograph him in different places. "He's been to Alaska, Hawaii, Gulf Shores, Alabama, and even Russia."

Tippy is not the only part of Turtle Run that visitors enjoy. The sense of fun there can be seen in the names of their wines such as Blue my Mind, Red my Mind, and Lost my Mind. Owner and wine maker, Pfeiffer follows the European laws to make sweet wines without added sugar compared to traditional American sweet wine making with added sugar or juice.

"Arrested fermentation wines, in which we stop fermentation, can lead to wines with half the sugar calories at the same sweetness as wines with added sugar," Pfeiffer emphasized. "Additionally, with the abundant flavors in wines, it's interesting to note that wines contain over 1,500 natural chemical compounds to express themselves.

Jim Pfeiffer's wine journey actually started in college, but it would be many years before it would lead him to wine making and winery ownership. "I took a wine appreciation class in college. The first day of the class, the professor announced, 'Who is here because you think you'll get to drink wine and it's an easy A?' When several people raised their hands, he asked them to leave and withdraw from the class." Never being one to shy away from a challenge, Pfeiffer was determined to get an A in a class where the average was a C-. He loved it. Always enamored with science, the math and precision behind wine making enthralled him? "In Burgundy, France, a few hundred yards could mean the difference between $2,000 per acre grapes and $9,000 per acre grapes."

When Pfeiffer began searching for a place in the US to grow grapes and start a winery, he looked for someplace where everyone wasn't doing the same thing. "No 'me too,' mentality," Pfeiffer said. The European model of grape growing uses no irrigation, which isn't feasible in many Western state growing areas in the US, and that is another caveat to his philosophy for making good wine. "It came down to Corydon, Indiana and Huntsville, Alabama. I got cold feet about Alabama and a little insect that may or may not be there."

Being a perfectionist at wine making has created a few situations that could have caused some problems. "There's one point where the fermenting process is perfect and the wine must be filtered to get all the yeast out within a three hour period. Some friends and family had planned a lovely anniversary dinner for my wife and me in the fermentation room. Everything had to be moved outside." Luckily, the weather was good and everyone understood his commitment as a wine maker to doing things when they need to be done. This perfection has served him well as the judges at the Indy International Wine Competition awarded him the 2014 trophy for Farm Winery of the Year, less than 50,000 bottles.

With wine and music events scheduled throughout the year, a variety of food items containing wine, picnic tables, a sundeck, playground equipment, and wonderful wines, there's something for everyone at Turtle Run Winery.

Note: Photographs for Turtle Run Winery were provided by Kathy Woodhouse.

Turtle Run Winery
940 St. Peters Church Road NE
Corydon, IN 47112
812-952-2650

Events: No

Trail: Indiana Uplands Wine Trail

259

Wines

❧ Cabernet Sauvignon

This full-bodied red is a customer favorite. Dark berry flavors aged in oak, this wine pairs perfectly with spaghetti and meatballs, braised lamb chops, or a beef brisket.

❧ Forever More

This oak aged crisp white is fruity and finishes smooth. Perfect to pair with shrimp or chicken scampi, raw oysters with hot sauce, or your favorite pasta and Alfredo sauce.

❧ Blue My Mind

Sweet and fruity, this fun red pairs well with barbecued chicken wings, meat topped pizzas, or chocolate cupcakes.

❧ Sweet Tortuga

This well-balanced wine contains citric tastes such as grapefruit and orange, but finishes on a sweet note. Pair with pork dishes, serve with your Thanksgiving dinner or serve at a garden party by mixing a can of frozen pink lemonade concentrate with one bottle of Sweet Tortuga.

From the Winery

Peach Wine Cake

1 cup Turtle Run Winery's Sweet Tortuga
1 box white cake mix
1 small box peach wine
1 cup vegetable oil
4 eggs
1 tsp. vanilla

Mix all ingredients together and pour into a greased Bundt or cake pan. Bake at 350° for 45 minutes or until cake tests done. While the cake is cooking, mix together glaze.

Glaze:
¼ cup Sweet Tortuga
1 ¾ cup powdered sugar

Mix together. It should be pourable, but not too thick. If it seems too thick, add wine a teaspoon at a time until desired consistency. Pour over cake while still hot. Cut and decorate however desired. We used peaches and pecans.

SCOUT MOUNTAIN WINERY & HIDEAWAY
CORYDON

"We have several 'porch wines.' Perfect to sip while sitting on the porch watching the sun go down."
– Mike Schad

Everything about Scout Mountain feels old and new at the same time. We made new friends; customers who explained their adventures with their first winemaking experience. "It tasted just like jet fuel." While owner Mike Schad, welcomed us like lifelong family, pouring wine and making sure all of our needs were met. Scout Mountain Winery is on the Hoosier Wine Trail and a steady stream of visitors came in to taste wine and get their passports stamped as we sipped and chatted.

"I became interested in wine making about 25 years ago when I tried someone's homemade wine," Schad explained. "I got curious about making my own." The wine bug bit and kind of took over. He took classes in enology and viticulture to gain confidence in his skill as a winemaker. The Schads first bought the 35 acres the winery sits on, to plant fruit trees. They decided to remodel the original 1920s farmhouse to make it a bed and breakfast and it didn't take long for the winery idea to fully develop. "We had an old barn on the property I didn't know what

to do with," Schad said. "A big storm came up and moved it about eight feet. It leaned badly and I didn't touch it until it fell down all the way." He then used some timbers and boards in the process of building the winery. Margaret and Mike Schad opened their winery and Bed and Breakfast, AKA The Hideaway, to the public in 2009.

Although wine is his main focus, it's not his only one. "We grow heirloom plants and vegetables that we use in recipes. Everything just tastes better. The tomatoes are juicier and have a thinner skin." They share their abundance with others, taking their products to farmer's markets and holding cooking and herb classes at the winery. Although the cooking classes are usually set up for bus tours that come to the winery, they will set up private classes for between 10 and 30 people. After tasting the Schad's cooking, we highly recommend the class. We also recommend a night or two stay in The Hideaway.

The bed and breakfast is spacious and has room for up to six guests. Visitors don't just have a room; they have a whole house that includes a back porch for Scout Mountain's porch wines and a hot tub. The Hideaway is secluded and private. Surrounded by the forest, guests may experience visits from deer, squirrels, and birds while enjoying the solitude. Being surrounded by all of this nature is something that influences the Schad's very much.

"The names of our wines come from local places and creatures, such as Blue River Blush, Hellbender, and Red Tail Hawk," Mike Schad said. A Hellbender is a peculiar species of salamander that many people have to see to believe. It's the largest species of salamander, growing up to two feet, and has rough skin and a flattened look. They only exist in a small portion of the US.

Whether your reason to visit is to get a stamp on the Hoosier Wine Trail, sip some porch wine, or stay at the Hideaway, Scout Mountain Winery is a must.

Note: Photographs for Scout Mountain Winery were provided by Kathy Woodhouse.

Scout Mountain Winery & Hideaway
2145 Scout Mountain Rd.
Corydon, IN 47112
812-738-7196
877-351-8607

Events: Yes, through the Hideaway. Indoors, up to 35. Outdoors, unlimited.

Trail: Hoosier Wine Trail

Wines

Buzzard Roost Red

A smooth Chambourcin wine aged in oak barrels. This wine is versatile and goes well with everything from a prime rib to meatloaf. Pairs especially well with tomato based sauces and dishes.

Vidal Blanc

This wonderful semi-dry white is refreshingly tangy with citrus tones. Pair with savory dishes, ham, and shellfish.

Red Tail Hawk

A sweet red with a cranberry tartness on the front that finishes with a hint of strawberries. A great addition to a sangria mixed with a container of frozen lemonade one cup of orange juice and two cups of ginger ale. Float oranges, lemons, and pineapple rings on top.

Apple Strawberry

A smooth porch sipping wine, this drink is mellow with a pop of tartness. Serve with chocolate covered strawberries, fruit tarts, or even a dish of salmon.

From the Winery

Pesto Salad

1 cup Fresh basil
½ cup Parmesan cheese
1 tsp. Garlic
¾ cup Olive oil
½ cup Walnuts
1 tsp. Lemon juice
Salt to taste
¾ lb. Feta noodles, cooked al dente

   In food processor, combine all ingredients, except feta noodles and process until smooth. Toss with feta noodles. Best served at room temperature. Pair with Scout Mountain Traminette.

WINZERWALD WINERY
BRISTOW

Winzerwald Winery (German for vintner of the forest) sits on fifty-five gently sloped acres in the Hoosier National Forest. Owners Dan and Donna Adams have had a clear vision of what they wanted for a winery for a long time; it would celebrate their German heritage. "Winemaking is in my blood," explained Dan. "My great-grandfather brought grape vines when he emigrated from Germany in the 1860s. He actually had a winery and was a barrel maker until prohibition. Legend has it he could change a bad stave in a barrel without losing a drop of wine." Even after Prohibition closed the winery, Dan's ancestors continued to grow grapes for personal use.

Dan's family has always lived in or near Evansville. He moved to Chicago after getting a law degree and met his wife Donna while working there she was originally from Wisconsin, and they quickly found a wine conection; Donna's family made wine too. When Donna's dad decided he did not want to make wine anymore, they transported several five gallon carboys from Wisconsin to their small condo in Chicago. Carboys are glass containers with

a narrow neck and small opening to make it easier to work with wine and other liquids. They started playing with winemaking as a hobby.

When Donna got a job offer in Wisconsin, they moved there. Dan had to retake the bar exam, which took some time, as the test is only offered once or twice a year. While waiting, he started working for a local winery, just to have something to do. Dan took and passed the bar, but decided to work at the winery a while longer. He never did go back to law. When Dan's father suggested they attend a meeting of the Indiana Winery and Vineyard Association (IWVA), the Adams were first introduced to commercial winemaking. The IWVA is compiled of people who are interested in grapes and winemaking, but don't necessarily own a winery or vineyard. Not long after, Donna and Dan, who both have certificates in enology and viticulture from the Heartland Wine School, decided to move to Indiana, grow grapes, and start a winery; Winzerwald opened in June of 2002.

The winery honors the German and Swiss roots in the area, which was founded by early German settlers

who thought the area resembled the Black Forest and the Ohio River was comparable to the Rhine. Donna chose their motif. "If we're going to be German," said Donna, "there's nothing more German than nutcrackers. Visitors looking around the winery will see nutcrackers of every shape, size and style. They give a cozy feel to the German modeled winery on top of the hill. The Adams offer German and Swiss style wines, with names such as Black Riesling, Schillerwein, Cranberry Weisser, and the popular Mai Wein. Local cheese is carried for guests to enjoy, including a personal favorite; apple pie cheddar. People can't help but notice the many medals around the tasting room.

In 1998, they won the Best Indiana and Best National Amateur wine awards at the Indy International Wine Competition. It was the first time anyone from Indiana won these accolades. The wine that won, a blush, was made from grapes the Adams' family has grown for years. It was rumored to have come from Germany with one of Dan's ancestors many years ago. Viticulture experts have been unable to identify the grape and the Adams refer to it as their "German Mystery Grape." They make a very limited edition wine from it called Heirloom.

In the words of the Adams, "The winery intends to serve top quality German and Swiss style wines and offer truly unique German and Swiss gift items at a fun, relaxing, educational and beautiful vineyard and winery locale. The tone is to be Olde World yet modern at the same time." We feel they've more than met this goal.

Winzerwald Winery
26300 North Indian Lake Road
Bristow, IN 47515
812-357-7000

Events: No

Trail: Indiana Uplands Wine Trail

Wines

Forest Red

Our semi-sweet red from Foch grapes has won several metals. Not too sweet or dry, this wine goes great with burgers, pizza, and pasta. If you like Chianti, be sure to try this one.

Riesling

This gold medal winner is light and not too sweet with flavors of mango and tropical fruits; pairs well with a variety of light foods.

Little Rhineland Blush

Silver medal winner at the Indy International Wine Competition, the well-balanced fruity blush blend matches well with ham, chicken, and turkey dishes.

Schweizer Spice

A gold medal winner, this spicy white wine is our "liquid pumpkin pie" with cinnamon – try with carrot cake, apple pie, or oriental dishes.

From the Winery

Dan Pusey's Honey Spiced Pork Loin with Winzerwald Glühwein

1 ½ cups of Winzerwald Glühwein Spiced Wine
3 pounds fresh pork loin
⅓ cup orange blossom, or similar, honey
¼ cup yellow mustard
¼ cup chopped garlic
Salt
Ground black pepper
Ground cyan seasonings
½ cup water
1 gallon freezer bag

Directions:

Lightly salt, pepper, and cyan the meat on all sides and then place the pork meat in a freezer bag and pour in the ¼ cup of the honey, ¼ cup of water, and the 1 ½ cups wine. Close the freezer bag, massage the meat, and place in the refrigerator in a flat baking dish for 12-24 hours. Massage the meat occasionally while in the refrigerator.

When ready to cook, preheat oven to 400° Place the pork loin in a hot iron skillet with some olive oil and braze all sides of the meat. Pour marinade into a roaster pan with the brazed pork loin. Add additional ¼ cup of water. Spread mustard over pork, and then drizzle the rest of the honey over it. Place chopped garlic on top, cover with foil, and bake for one hour. Turn the roast over, recover with foil, and turn the oven to 200° for 2-3 hours more.

Remove the pork loin to a wooden cutting board, cover with aluminum foil and let rest for 20 minutes. Slice or pull the pork loin. Serve with gravy made from pan drippings.

Simple Gravy:

Pour pan drippings into the iron skillet that was used for browning. (Note: If you are worried about too much pork fat, place the liquid in a bowl and place in the freezer to solidify the fat for removal.) Make a roux of ⅛ – ¼ cup of flour with cold water in a separate dish. Heat the liquid to a slight boil and add the roux, stir and return the liquid to a boil. Salt and pepper to taste. This is a great sauce for pork loin or over mashed potatoes. Serve with a glass of Winzerwald Glühwein Spiced Wine or Winzerwald Blaufränkisch.

MONKEY HOLLOW WINERY
ST. MEINRAD

While sitting on the porch of Monkey Hollow Winery's red barn-like tasting room, visitors can sip their favorite wine while looking out over the beautiful landscaping, vineyards, and down to a very small creek that gives this winery its unique name. "We looked at historical maps," said Faye Hedinger, one of the part-owners. "We found that the little creek that divides the farm was called 'Monkey Hollow Ditch,' we dropped the ditch."

Guests will find three generations at both locations of Monkey Hollow at any given time. Everyone in the family tends to the vineyards, Anita Hedinger or Jamie Zellers run the tasting bar throughout the week, and Daniel Hedinger II is the winemaker. On the day we visited, little Vera danced around as she told us about her birthday three days away. When asked her favorite part of the winery, she whispered conspiratorially, "When I get to help out and when my mom makes cookies for the winery." Monkey Hollow participates in several events along the Hoosier Wine Trail including Chocolate Weekends in February, which was the reason for Vera's happy dance. Whatever season, the focus of the winery is local.

"For building the winery, a local farmer harvested the wood and dried it himself," emphasized Faye.

Cheeses, meats, and artwork are all provided from within twenty miles of the winery. They have musicians every Saturday in the summer, which bring in a lot of crowds. "We're focused on making this a local hub of activity," said Faye. Even the logo was decided locally. "We held a contest at Indiana University to come up with the name and logo for the winery, then hired the winner. She's now at a design firm in Chicago, but will still freelance for us." Some of the names of the wine help to further tell the story of Monkey Hollow Winery.

"Pasture White, Pasture Red, and Pasture Limit, are so named because the winery is built on part of a former cow pasture," explained Faye. Daniel Sr. continues to breed and raise cattle on the 132 acres that also contains the winery and vineyards. In the early 2000s, when it became time to downsize somewhat, Dan Sr., his wife Anita, and their children Tammy Sturgeon, Jaime Zellers, Andy Hedinger, and Dan Jr. (and spouse Faye), all agreed they wanted to keep the land in the family. Dan's kids and their spouses decided to grow grapes because they wanted to continue in the agricultural business, but wanted to grow something different than the corn or soybeans typically grown in the area. The owners of Monkey Hollow put the land into an LLC and started growing grapes to sell while Dan Jr. learned to make wine through books, conferences, and advice from others. They kept the 2010 harvest and opened the winery in 2011. In 2014 they expanded, opening a new location called Monkey Hollow Winery & Bistro at the Wollenmann Home. This location is not a tasting room, but their wines are available at the bar or in the restaurant. In addition to the winery and bistro, all of Monkey Hollow's owners have other full-time jobs so there isn't much time on anyone's hands. One would think that would be enough, but they've always got their eye out for the next thing. Their latest "next thing" is a distillery.

"We're covering the alcohol market in two counties," Faye laughed as she told that her brother-in-law Andy Hedinger and a partner recently opened a brewery that is separate from the winery and distillery. Monkey Hollow's recently opened distillery's first offering is a white whiskey called Monkey Shine and it will soon be followed by gin, vodka, fruit liqueurs and eventually, whiskey.

Whatever passion visitors might have, be it food, wine, distilled spirits or nature, they couldn't find a better place to spend an afternoon than Monkey Hollow Winery.

Monkey Hollow Winery
11534 E County Road 170 N
St. Meinrad, IN 47577
812-357-2272

Second Location:
Monkey Hollow Winery & Bistro
  at the Wollenmann Home
1050 Main Street
Ferdinand, IN 47532
812-998-2112

Events: Yes, indoors up to 100;
  outdoors, up to 200

Trail: Hoosier Wine Trail

Wines

- ### Chambourcin
  A dry red with an intense deep red color and flavor to match. Fully aromatic with hints of plum and blackberry. Pair with fatty grilled fish, such as tuna, roasted chicken, and spicy lamb curry.

- ### Pasture Mark
  A Catawba Rosé aged in a Kentucky bourbon barrel, this smooth sipping wine pairs well with scallops and shellfish.

- ### Pasture White
  Our flagship sweet wine made from the ever fruity Cayuga White grapes. Enjoy chilled on a hot summer day.

Pairing

We like Monkey Hollow Winery's Chardonel because it goes with so many foods. Save it for an appetizer party with plenty of cheeses such as the Port Style Merlot Cheese Ball on page 179 (Salt Creek Winery) or the Lily White Teasers on page 249. (Indian Creek Winery)

MYSTIQUE WINERY
LYNNVILLE

"Where friends meet and the wine is unique."
– The Clutters

Walking out onto the back patio at Mystique Winery, visitors will feel as if they've been transported to an Italian Villa. The black tables and chairs offer a lot of seating areas. The stone walls with beautiful landscaping surround the patio, which overlooks a clear lake. Spring, summer and fall, people gather to share good times and camaraderie in a place designed for guests' comfort.

Mystique is a family owned winery imagined by the Clutter family. Steve and Patti Clutter and their sons and daughters-in-laws, Seth and Heather, Zeb and Jennifer, started making wine together just for fun. They would

taste each other's creations and offer advice to make the wines better. Seth has a chemistry background and liked trying to perfect wine.

The place where the winery sits is part of the Clutter family homestead. The family wanted something the entire family could do on the ground and make it productive. They all wanted to keep it agricultural, but wanted to grow a cash crop. They kicked around the idea of growing corn or soybeans, but with their interest in wine, it wasn't long before they decided to plant grapes. Instead of just selling grapes to other

wineries, Steve and Patti, Seth and Heather, and Zeb and Jen discussed the idea of opening a winery. All of them were working full-time jobs when they planted their first vines.

"We'd been going to wineries since the 1970s," said Steve. "My parents had a tavern in Buckskin (a small town in Indiana). We liked going to wineries because everybody had a story to tell." In November of 2012, the Clutters opened the first winery in Warrick County, a spot sitting in the gently rolling hills of Southern Indiana.

The cute tasting room is a dedication to their love of everything Mardi Gras. They regularly take trips to New Orleans and soak in all of the culture while there. Many of the decorations and gift shop items are a reflection of this. Even some of their wines are named after Mardi Gras Krewes. There are more than fifty Krewes that organize people to come together and host a Mardi Gras ball, ride on a parade float, and participate in social events. This isn't done only the month of February; the social events are throughout the year and help to raise money for the February parties. King Rex and Zulu are just of few of Krewe examples. In the spirit of giving that is Mardi Gras, the people at Mystique Winery are very generous with their winery and their time.

Every June, they host a Cajun Fest Benefit for local animal shelters. There are four bands and local organizers come in and make Cajun foods and artists display their work. This event is very popular and they suggest you bring a chair to enjoy the festivities. Mystique Winery and their donors were able to help seven separate shelters from last year's event. Mystique is also one of the sponsors of Animalpalooza, a two-day festival every year, usually in September, that features dog competitions, many bands and musicians, food, car shows, and other surprises. The event is held at Burdette Park in Evansville.

Mystique Winery would love for you to come and visit them soon. "We love the socializing and making new friends," Patti said. "We thrive on a good customer experience." They welcome you to come and be part of that experience.

Mystique Winery
13000 Gore Road
Lynnville, IN 47619
812-922-5612

Events: No

Trail: Hoosier Wine Trail

Hours: Wed-Thur-Sat-Sun (11-6) Fri (11-8) CST

Wines

King Rex

This semi-sweet Riesling wine is crisp and fruity. It pairs well with snappy flavors, lime, jalapeño, and tomatillo in fish and Spanish dishes.

Hoosier Red

This semi-sweet Chambourcin wine is smooth with earthy tones. Medium-bodied with a fruity finish, pair with grilled fish or roast chicken. Also works well with beef and lamb.

Zulu

Black cherry noir describes the sweet red wine with a strong hit of cherries. Drink as a dessert wine, pour over cheesecake, or add to a cobbler for an extra zing.

Carnival

A fruity white wine blend, this sweet Chardonnay has stunning hints of peach and floral notes. Chill for a delicious summer drink or use as a marinade for pork or chicken.

From the Winery

Mystique Moscato Ice Cream

1 ½ cups Mystique Moscato Wine
1 tsp vanilla
½ cup sugar
2 ½ cups heavy whipping cream
Blackberry dessert wine or port
Blackberries for garnish

Directions:

In a large bowl, mix Moscato wine and vanilla together with mixer. Add in heavy whipping cream and mix at high speed. Slowly add sugar and continue mixing at high speed until mixture becomes slightly stiff. Pour into rectangular container and freeze until firm; 3-4 hours or overnight. Scoop ice cream into a tall glass. Garnish with blackberries and drizzle with blackberry dessert wine or port.

HEDGEGROVE FARMS MEADERY AND WINERY
CYNTHIANA

Many of the roads in this part of Indiana are still gravel and the stir of nostalgia rises along them as well as the dust of the past. Just past the crossroads of County Road 800 and 1000 sits Hedgegrove Meadery and Winery. Opening in 2013, their meadery, a winery producing wine from honey, is in the process of opening a tasting room. Until then, their meads and wines can be ordered online, enjoyed at many Indiana wine festivals, or found at farmer's markets in the Evansville and Indianapolis area. They can also be found in wine shops, grocers, and restaurants across the state of Indiana.

Although Nathan and Laura Kluger now call this nearly two hundred year old house their home, they both are worldwide travelers. "I majored in business with a large focus on the natural sciences," said Nathan. "I decided to go to China and see the world." Laura grew up in Ecuador and had quite a circuitous route before settling in Cynthiana. "We met in China," said Nathan, "while both of us were there teaching English." For many years after returning to the states, Nathan was the proprietor of the iconic Newburgh General Store, founded by his grandfather, Kurt Kluger. The store was a staple for fifty years, selling homemade products, culinary herbs, honey, old fashioned candy, old-world style wooden toys and many other treasures. The family made the decision to close the general store in 2013.

The Klugers had a plan, but it took them a while to make everything come together. "We've wanted to be close to the earth for a long time," explained Nathan. "It took us a long time to find this place." The place he spoke of is the lovely home and grounds he and his wife found in 2008. There was a salt trace that

bison followed. Early Americans followed the bison trails for hunting, and roads followed these natural paths. The area was settled between 1815 and 1830. "In the attic, we found letters sent here in 1821," said Laura. The Klugers have been working on fixing and restoring their home and still have much work to do. Along with this, they're learning the business of making wine and mead.

"We started with a dry wine," explained Nathan. "The area is an Old German area and the German palate is geared more toward the sweet wines. Mead, with its historical roots, was a perfect fit. Another reason it was a perfect fit is the experience the Klugers have with honey. Nathan's father, Robert, produced honey for shops and restaurants and sold it at their general store. He gave Nathan his first hive and still consults with him. The two apiaries he has now can produce between 3,000 and 5,000 pounds of honey a year. Another Kluger family member who had a big influence on Nathan was his grandmother, Marylin Kluger.

"She was a food writer for *Gourmet Magazine* and other publications, as well as a published author of several cookbooks," said Nathan. "She'd let me in the kitchen and let me pull out things and be creative." We received the benefit of this experience when Nathan prepared the pear recipe below for us. "I guess my grandmother rubbed off on me," Nathan laughed. "And I get the benefit of it," interjected Laura. "He loves trying new recipes. He makes sweets and doesn't care for them. He makes them just for me."

Laura loves their visits to Grandmother Kluger's. "She's a wellspring of information. She's visited England a lot. She's well-read and grew up on a farm in Southern Indiana. She has great stories surrounding this."

The love of family, the land, and making and trying new things can be experienced by all who come to visit with the Klugers. They will soon have a tasting room open so that all can come and experience their wonderful hospitality and beautiful landscape.

Note: Photographs for Hedgegrove Farms were provided by Kathy Woodhouse.

Hedgegrove Farms Meadery and Winery
8780 South 800 West
Cynthiana, IN 47612
812-962-0922

Events: No, but hope to eventually

Unfortunately, on February 28th, 2017, an F-4 tornado hit Hedgrove Farms and did extensive damage. The Klugers are in the process of rebuilding. Please call before planning a visit.

Wines

❧ Soft Summer Blush
A semi-sweet black currant mead that pairs with almost any cuisine. Sever chilled.

❧ Sweet Summer Mead
Made exclusively from our own apiary's raw melon honey, this delicate sweet mead balances delicate floral and citrus aromas from the honey. An excellent pairing with Asian cuisines.

❧ Blue Summer Solstice Blueberry Mead
This blueberry mead is delicately sweet with a touch of blueberry. Perfect for roast game and grilled vegetables.

❧ Raspberry Silhouette
Fruity raspberry aromas blossom along with the natural honey bouquet of this delightful sparkling mead. Pair with salads, fresh cheeses, or drink on its own.

From the Winery

Hedgegrove Pears

4 Fresh ripe Bosc Pears, Halved and cored
½ cup Brandy
½ cup Hedgegrove Sweet Summer Mead
1 Tbls. white sugar
4-8 small Cinnamon Sticks
¾ tsp. cornstarch + ¼ cup water
½ cup Mascarpone
½ tsp. fresh ground nutmeg
1 Tbls. dark Brown Sugar
½ tsp. Madagascar Bourbon Vanilla
Zest of orange , garnish (optional)
3-5 Tbls. fresh raw honey

Add brandy, mead, sugar, cinnamon sticks to a pan and place pears in pan. Bring to a simmer. Baste pears often and simmer on low until pears begin to soften, approximately 10-15 minutes. Remove pears and place each on their own dish. Thicken the remaining liquid with the cornstarch and water mixture and continue to simmer and reduce the sauce. When the sauce has thickened, ladle equal portions on top of each pear and divide the cinnamon sticks among the pears. Allow to cool, cover with plastic wrap and refrigerate at least 6 hours.

Mix the Mascarpone with the nutmeg, brown sugar, and vanilla and beat until smooth. Reserve for the pears.

When the pears have chilled, remove plastic wrap and spoon the raw honey over the top of the pears as a glaze. Serve with the mascarpone and zest of an orange (optional).

LITTLE CREEK WINERY
EVANSVILLE

"Enjoy the experience"
– The Ripplemeiers

One of the newer wineries on the block, Little Creek Winery is the first winery to open in Vanderburgh County. Little Creek has a small stream on the property that runs into Big Creek; thus the name Little Creek. Completely family owned and operated, this home farm winery offers a variety of dry and sweet wines in both red and white, as well as other fruit wines.

When entering the property, the first thing that catches your eye is the cute tasting room building, with its weather vane, front porch, and colorful Adirondack chairs. An old time dinner bell, sits near the entrance, giving the winery a neat farmhouse look. The next thing you notice is the vineyards stretching out toward a pond. The view sitting on the deck, with its metal chairs and cheery red umbrellas, is not to be missed. The peaceful atmosphere makes one forget that Evansville, the third largest city in Indiana, is just a few miles away. Owners Alan and Sharon Ripplemeier have worked hard to make a welcoming space for their many visitors, but it took several years before the idea first hit that they might want to own a winery.

Their daughter Christy can be found helping out at the winery most Saturdays and told the story of Little Creek Winery. "Dad started making wine when he was 21 and never stopped. I can remember he always had something fermenting," she laughed. For recreation, they would take motorcycle rides to wineries and be-

came interested in all processes surrounding owning a winery. It became a bucket list item. In 2007, Alan planted his first 150 grape vines at his home. Also in 2007, Sharon and Alan acquired some land on the west side of Evansville and planted another 2,000 vines. By 2014, they were ready to build their winery.

Both of the Ripplemeiers "retired" before starting the winery. Alan was in facilities management. He also oversaw the building of some public schools. Sharon was a teacher. They have always had a love of gardening and building things. The life experiences

Little Creek Winery
4116 Koressel Road
Evansville, IN 47720
812-480-2832

of the two morphed perfectly into their winery hobby and they turned to this love of family heritage and the land when building the winery. A large cherry tree from Sharon's uncle's farm became the top of the tasting bar. Her uncle had told Alan if he'd help take the tree down, he could have some of the wood. He took it and kept it in his barn for many years until he found just the right project. He pulled it out for the winery. Alan also built all of the cabinets in the winery.

One thing they really insist on for their wine is that it all comes from their vines. They have fifteen acres with five planted in several grape varieties including Chambourcin, Cayuga, White, Catawba, Concord, Norton, Traminette, Steuben, and Niagara. Five acres of grapes may not sound like much, but one acre of grapes can produce up to around 1,200 bottles of wine. The Ripplemeires expect to bottle about 1,500 gallons this year. Alan makes all of the wine himself in the wine-making facility there on the property with family and friends, helping whenever needed.

Although many wineries are constantly growing and always looking for the next building project, Little Creek Winery prefers to stay small. Since this is a hobby for Alan, the focus is on making good wine and having great customer service. This is witnessed by any visitors who enter the doors of Little Creek Winery. We highly suggest you take a trip to visit soon.

Wines

❧ Chambourcin Rosé

This dry wine is light-bodied and estate grown. It pairs well with savory pepper dishes, spicy Thai, and is a natural for baked ham.

❧ Sunset Red

A semi-sweet red wine made from estate grown Steuben grapes. This one pairs with all the comfort foods, especially a savory pork roast with mashed potatoes and gravy.

❧ Niagara

A sweet white wine with grape flavor that bursts in your mouth. It's wonderful in a punch or sangria. Pair with summer fruits and vegetables.

❧ Concord

Most likely the best well known American grape, this wine is very popular. Mix with some semi-sweet chocolate, mix half and half with lemon-lime soda, or drink alone.

From the Winery

Niagara Mango Sangria

One bottle Little Creek Niagara
¼ cup of sugar
½ cup of white grape juice
½ cup mango nectar (or substitute another frozen nectar of choice)
Slices of frozen mango

Mix room temperature juice and sugar together until sugar is dissolved. Add chilled wine and frozen nectar. Stir until nectar melts. Place a few slices of frozen mango in a glass and pour sangria over it. Serve.

Visitors to Pepper's Ridge Winery will find it pays homage to many of the things important in the lives of owners Kevin and Micki DeWeese. The name itself comes from the nickname for Kevin's father and grandfather. A rare wooden canoe over the tasting bar is a nod to the sport of fishing, enjoyed by many family members. Even the names of the wines reflect the love of being in natural surroundings. Photos of family members, along with various memorabilia from western movies, shelves of pottery jugs, and the hunting and fishing world, cover the log walls. All have their

individual stories and give Pepper's Ridge the feel of a hunting or fishing cabin, but the canoe is one of the best tales to be heard.

"It's a 1948 Trapper handmade canoe from Maine," explained Kevin. "My best friend was a car dealer in Atlanta, and someone gave it to him as a trade-in on a car. I wouldn't take anything for it." The DeWeese's believe in repurposing nostalgic items. The beams came from a friend's barn that was built in the 1890s and feed sacks hanging on the walls give a nod to the agricultural roots of the area. Even the building blends in well with the surrounding area.

The rustic red Morton building that houses the tasting room is often filled with visitors sampling the unique wines at Pepper's Ridge. The names honor DeWeese's outdoorsman roots. Bird Dog Blues, Lock and Load persimmon, and Lakeview Peach, are just a few of the many wines at this gem of a winery. "I make country wines," explained DeWeese. "Peach, blueberry, raspberry, elderberry," plants that grow naturally in the wild.

Musicians, much to the delight of guests, entertain every weekend. The picnic tables on the picturesque property are usually filled with people enjoying Pepper's Ridge wines and foods they've brought with them. No outside alcohol is allowed on the property. Looking at his successful winery, it may be surprising to some that Kevin DeWeese never planned to open a winery.

Although he'd experimented with wine making since the 1980s, he never seriously considered turning it into a business. "I heard about the auction of the property the day before it happened. At 5:30 in the morning, I walked the property and I bought it at 10:30." Kevin's reasoning for this was more because of family history rather than a business. They now have six generations that have lived in Spencer County, Indiana. After buying the property, the thought of opening a winery began to appeal to him more. "I wanted to open a business that will keep my grandchildren in the area. I was lucky that right out of high school, Alcoa Aluminum hired me." DeWeese's life is one surrounded by high expectations for himself, his wines, and his employees.

"I hire quality people from this community. Quality people give quality work." Employees include a teacher and a librarian and both owners and employees all have a deep mutual respect for each other. Although the bar is often surrounded by people three deep, DeWeese does not want the winery to get any bigger. "I want to run a business; I don't want a business to run me." We urge you to come and visit the picturesque surroundings at Pepper's Ridge. Bring some food and friends and relax in the country atmosphere. We guarantee you'll be back.

Note: Photographs for Pepper's Ridge Winery were provided by Kathy Woodhouse.

Pepper's Ridge Winery
4304 North County Road 200 West, Rockport, IN 47635
812-649-9463

Events: Yes, call for details

Trail: Hoosier Wine Trail

Wines

✤ Small Town White (Paw-Paw)
Smooth, fruity, and juicy, this dry wine has the hint of paw-paws and pairs well with game birds.

✤ Knob Hill Quencher (Foch)
Semi-dry and full-bodied, this wine pairs well with tuna, a spicy jambalaya or gumbo, and broccoli dishes.

✤ Cowboy Up White (Pineapple)
The taste of pineapple lingers on the tongue after sipping this semi-sweet wine. Great for slushies. Freeze in an aluminum pie pan. Scrape into wine glass. Finish off with whipped topping, toasted coconut, and a cherry.

✤ Raspberry (Red)
Smooth and tart, this is a great wine to add to pies and cobblers or pour over ice cream.

Recipe

Wine-a-colada

2 cups Pepper's Ridge Cowboy Up White
  wine
One can frozen pineapple juice
One can frozen Pina Colada mix
One banana

Combine all ingredients in blender. Garnish with pineapple and an umbrella. Enjoy!

BLUE HERON VINEYARDS AND WINERY
CANNELTON

"A Rock • A Vine • A Vision"
– Gary and Lynn Dauby

Standing on the deck at Blue Heron Vineyards and Winery, visitors will view one of the prettiest sights they're likely to find anywhere in the world. Sun glistens off the water and fall leaves drift on the wind as they sip their favorite wines in the natural surroundings. Situated on a slight bend on the Ohio River, Blue Heron has much to offer for anyone who ventures to the winery.

Owners Gary and Lynn Dauby are most welcoming hosts. Both have degrees in education and have impacted an untold amount of people throughout their lives. Gary has taught at the elementary, junior high, and high school levels, ending up in prison; teaching that is. When he finally decided to retire, he was the Education Administer at Branchville Correctional Center.

Lynn's focus has always been toward the art world. After thirty-three years of teaching art in Tell City and Perry Central Community Schools, Lynn "retired" to create projects at Blue Heron. She paints with acrylics, watercolors, and pastels and her Victorian-style Santas on slate and barn wood have become collectors' items. You can view these, as well as walking sticks created by Gary and other local artisans, at Blue Heron's gift shop. This penchant for art can also be seen in one of the highlights of Blue Heron Vineyards and Winery; the stone-carved Celtic Cross sculpture.

A local craftsman, Greg Harris, spent almost two years creating a High Celtic Cross, the oldest cross

290

in Ireland, within a large, natural stone on a hillside on Blue Heron's property. Spending hours on the project, morning to night, six days a week, whatever the weather, he carved the sculpture into the impressive form it is today. Though unsure, Harris and the Daubys believe it to be the largest in situ in the world. In situ is a term meaning in its original place. A number of almost mystical happenings surround the cross. The number 23 is repeated many times in both the design and measurements to complete the design. The 23rd psalm is important to the understanding of faith in God. The sculpture is built on prime numbers and is a model for the "Golden Mean" or Ratio. The Golden Mean is a measurement seen in both art and architecture, but it also shows up in nature. One of the most amazing things about the cross, however, may be that Greg Harris has no formal training. When asked how he knows what to do to create his art, he says, "I don't know, I just know." The cross is so important to the Daubys, they've had a bronze replica made so that people who are blind can touch it and get an idea what it looks like. A short trek leads visitors to the cross and nearly every person who visits, goes there to take photos in the lovely spot.

Blue Heron Vineyards and Winery
5330 Blue Heron Lane
Cannelton, IN 47520
812-547-7518

Events: Yes, outdoors, up to 100.

Trail: Hoosier Wine Trail

The Daubys recently added a rental cottage within walking distance of the winery. The same rustic, but artistic, eye seen in the winery carries through its two bedrooms, great room with a kitchen, and wrap-around porch with views as majestic as the winery.

The day we were there, we met John and Patty Burkhardt, who are on a mission to visit all of the wineries in Indiana. They are between seven and eight years into their journey and have visited about 3/4ths of them. "We've gotten to know the owners and they let us try wines they are in the process of making. We just love to meander the state."

We love to meander the state too. While visiting wineries, tasting their offerings, and meeting all of the fine owners, such as the Daubys, we understand commitment to family traditions, agriculture, and the customer. Sláinte! (Cheers in Gaelic.)

Wines

❧ Twin Towers Red (Red Cap)

Made from locally grown Chambourcin grapes this dry red wine is fruity and lightly oaked. Pour a cup in your favorite pot of chili or vegetable soup.

❧ 23 Degrees

Indiana grown Villard Noir and DeChaunac grapes dance in this medium-dry red wine with hints of plum. Serve with a brunch quiche or frittata.

❧ On Deck Red (Blue Capsule)

This sweet wine is best sipped while relaxing on one of our decks perched high above the banks of the Ohio River. Pair with chocolate.

❧ On Deck White

Made from local grapes, this white wine is light and refreshing with the sweetness of honeysuckle with a slightly dry finish. Blend in a spritzer.

Recipe

Asian Sesame Chicken

½ cup Blue Heron On Deck White Wine
1 cup Light Asian Sesame Salad Dressing
1 tsp onion powder
1 teaspoon garlic powder
¼ cup Worcestershire sauce
pinch of salt
pinch of ground pepper
4 or 5 thawed boneless chicken breast.

Directions:

Place chicken breasts in a 1 gallon plastic bag with zipper top, add all the ingredients, seal the bag and mix well. Refrigerate for at least 8 hours, turning the bag occasionally. Fire up the grill and cook the chicken until cooked through and no pink remains.

Other Wineries

AFTERMATH CIDERY AND WINERY
454 Greenwich
Valparaiso, IN 46383
(219) 390-9463

ASH & ELM CIDER CO
2104 E. Washington St.
Indianapolis, IN 46201
(317) 600-3164

BYLER LANE WINERY
5858 County Rd 35
Auburn, IN 46706
(260) 920-4377

DANIEL'S VINEYARD
9061 N. 700 W.
McCordsville, IN 46055
(877) 994-7273

FRUITSHINE WINERY
11752 W 1100 N.
Monticello, IN 47960
(574) 808-9229

HARTLAND WINERY
425 County Rd. 23
Ashley, IN 46705
(260) 668-5324

HEAGY VINEYARDS
9424 N 700 W.
Roann, IN 46974
(317) 752-4779

IRONHAND VINEYARD
21481 Brick Rd.
South Bend IN 46383
(574) 360-5388

LAMBSTONE CELLARS
1555 West Lincolnway, Suite 1
Valparaiso, IN 46347

MISSBEHAVIN MEADS
65 Franklin St.
Valparaiso, IN 46383
(219) 242-8616

NEW DAY CRAFT
1102 Prospect St. Historic Fountain Sq.
Indianapolis, IN 46203
(888) 632-3799

OAK HILL WINERY
111 E. Marion St.
Converse, IN 46919
(765) 395-3632

PEACE WATER WINERY
37 W. Main St.
Carmel, IN 46032
(317) 810-1330

RETTIG HILL WINERY
Visit website to see where wines are sold
robertpesce.com/rettighill

RUNNING VINES WINERY
119 S Calumet
Chesterton, IN 46304
(219) 390-9463

SMITH'S WINERY
6090 E 100 S.
Columbus, IN 47201
(812) 372-4548

TIPPY CREEK WINERY
5998 N 200 E.
Leesburg, IN 46538
(574) 529-0649

About the Author

Author Becky Kelley has been a freelance writer since 2003 and published in many magazines, newspapers, and anthologies. In addition, she has won several writing competitions and taught English and writing at the college level. She has a self-published children's book, *A Tail of Christmas.* Her first non-fiction book, *Wineing Your Way Across Kentucky*, was published by Acclaim Press in April of 2015. Becky is currently working on a true crime mystery with two writing friends, Jean Kinsey and Diane Theiler. She also has a mystery series in production. A lifelong Bullitt Countian, she graduated from North Bullitt High School, Spalding University, and The University of Louisville, respectively. She lives by the motto, "Learn something new every day."

About the Photographers

Wineing Your Way Across Indiana is the first book project for back-up photographer Molly Kelley, but she has had a love of the arts her entire life. She's won awards at both the state and national level for her writing and photography, and is working on a children's book specifically for autistic individuals. Molly believes that peoples' love of arts can help anyone find common ground. She's unsure of what direction this new adventure will take her, but she's excited to see where it goes. She lives with her soon to be husband, Tyler, three cats, Oliver, Six, (for his six toes) and Wednesday, and one hamster, Kahlua. She's a graduate of North Bullitt High School and has plans to take classes to further her knowledge of photography.

Kathy Woodhouse, photographer of *Wineing Your Way Across Kentucky* and *Wineing Your Way Across Indiana*, has been photographing professionally for more than three decades. Her experience has spanned a myriad of styles including studio, retail, and managing multi-unit retail where she taught photography, managed personnel, and trained studio management. Amongst her many accolades, Kathy was named National Sears Portrait Studio Manager of the Year. In addition, her work was featured on NBC's *Today Show*, December 13, 2013. For the last decade, Kathy has owned her own studio and worked as a freelance photojournalist, marketing her work at various galleries and retail outlets in Kentucky. Kathy is a proud native of Kentucky and Bullitt County and is a graduate of North Bullitt High School. She also attended Elizabethtown Community College and is certified in both photography and Graphic Arts.

Index of Wineries

Index of Recipes

Side Items

Soups

Salads

Sweets & Desserts